Intelligence and Abilities

'Engages in critical evaluation using language and style that is accessible to students'

John Todman, *University of Dundee*

'Ideal for undergraduates taking the Individual Differences and Cognitive Psychology modules . . . conveys complex theories clearly and well.'

Linda Thompson, *graduate student,*
University of Westminster

Intelligence and Abilities is written for non-specialists and explains what is known about the structure and processes associated with mental abilities, and their relationship with behaviour outside the laboratory. Five topics are considered. First, what abilities are, how they are distinct from personality traits and other forms of individual differences and how factor analysis has been used to explore their structure. Second, Colin Cooper considers and evaluates the theories of Sternberg, Gardner and Howe, who eschew the method of factor anlaysis, and then considers evidence for and against a genetic interpretation of general ability. The fourth section explores what is known about the links between abilities, cognition and the biology of the nervous system; the book concludes by looking at the extent to which scores on ability tests are related to real-life behaviour.

Colin Cooper is Lecturer in Psychology at the Queen's University, Belfast. He has taught and published extensively in the field of individual differences. He has recently edited *Processes in Individual Differences* (Routledge 1997) and authored a textbook on the nature and measurement of individual differences.

Psychology Focus

Series editor: Perry Hinton, University of Luton

The Psychology Focus series provides students with a new focus on key topic areas in psychology. It supports students taking modules in psychology, whether for a psychology degree or a combined programme, and those renewing their qualification in a related discipline. Each short book:

- presents clear, in-depth coverage of a discrete area with many applied examples
- assumes no prior knowledge of psychology
- has been written by an experienced teacher
- has chapter summaries, annotated further reading and a glossary of key terms.

Also available in this series:

Being Ill (forthcoming)
Marian Pitts

Friendship in Childhood and Adolescence
Phil Erwin

Gender and Social Psychology
Vivien Burr

Jobs, Technology and People
Nik Chmiel

Learning and Studying
James Hartley

Personality: A Cognitive Approach
Jo Brunas-Wagstaff

Psychobiology of Human Motivation
Hugh Wagner

Stereotypes, Social Cognition and Culture
Perry Hinton

Stress, Cognition and Health
Tony Cassidy

Types of Thinking
S. Ian Robertson

Intelligence and Abilities

■ Colin Cooper

LONDON AND NEW YORK

First published 1999
by Routledge
11 New Fetter Lane, London
EC4P 4EE

© 1999 Colin Cooper

Typeset in Sabon and Futura by
The Florence Group, Stoodleigh,
Devon

Printed and bound in Great Britain by
Creative, Print and Design (Wales),
Ebbw Vale

*British Library Cataloguing in
Publication Data*
A catalogue record for this book is
available from the British Library

*Library of Congress Cataloging in
Publication Data*
Cooper, Colin, 1954–
  Intelligence and abilities / Colin
Cooper.
    p.   cm. – (Psychology focus)
  Includes bibliographical references
  and index
  1. Intellect.   2. Human behavior.
  I. Title.   II. Series.
  BF431.C665   1999
  153.9—dc21   98–42127
                                      CIP

ISBN 0–415–18868–7 (hbk)
ISBN 0–415–18869–5 (pbk)

Contents

CONTENTS

Figures

Tables

Series preface

The Psychology Focus series provides short, up-to-date accounts of key areas in psychology without assuming the reader's prior knowledge in the subject. Psychology is often a favoured subject area for study, since it is relevant to a wide range of disciplines such as Sociology, Education, Nursing and Business Studies. These relatively inexpensive but focused short texts combine sufficient detail for psychology specialists with sufficient clarity for non-specialists.

The series authors are academics experienced in undergraduate teaching as well as research. Each takes a key topic within their area of psychological expertise and presents a short review, highlighting important themes and including both theory and research findings. Each aspect of the topic is clearly explained with supporting glossaries to elucidate technical terms.

The series has been conceived within the context of the increasing modularisation which has been developed in higher education over the last decade

and fulfils the consequent need for clear, focused, topic-based course material. Instead of following one course of study, students on a modularisation programme are often able to choose modules from a wide range of disciplines to complement the modules they are required to study for a specific degree. It can no longer be assumed that students studying a particular module will necessarily have the same background knowledge (or lack of it!) in that subject. But they will need to familiarise themselves with a particular topic since a single module in a single topic may be only fifteen weeks long, with assessments arising during that period. They may have to combine eight or more modules in a single year to obtain a degree at the end of their programme of study.

One possible problem with studying a range of separate modules is that the relevance of a particular topic or the relationship between topics may not always be apparent. In the Psychology Focus series authors have drawn where possible on practical and applied examples to support the points being made so that readers can see the wider relevance of the topic under study. Also, the study of psychology is usually broken up into separate areas, such as social psychology, developmental psychology and cognitive psychology, to take three examples. Whilst the books in the Psychology Focus series will provide excellent coverage of certain key topics within these 'traditional' areas, the authors have not been constrained in their examples and explanations and may draw on material across the whole field of psychology to help explain the topic under study more fully.

Each text in the series provides the reader with a range of important material on a specific topic. They are suitably comprehensive and give a clear account of the important issues involved. The authors analyse and interpret the material as well as present an up-to-date and detailed review of key work. Recent references are provided along with suggested further reading to allow readers to investigate the topic in more depth. It is hoped, therefore, that after following the informative review of a key topic in a Psychology Focus text, readers not only will have a clear understanding of the issues in question but also will be intrigued and challenged to investigate the topic further.

Mental abilities

THE PSYCHOLOGY OF ABILITY is a branch of psychology that examines how and why people differ from one another – as opposed to other areas of the discipline which regard such 'individual differences' as nuisances, to be ignored (or controlled for statistically) in psychology experiments. For example, social psychology studies variables that influence prejudice *in the population*, and does not trouble to consider whether or why some individuals are more prejudiced against minority groups than others. **Cognitive psychologists** try to draw inferences about neural mechanisms by studying how various features of stimuli influence response time; they are rarely interested in whether or why some individuals perform more quickly or slowly than the norm in *all* experimental conditions. Thus Cronbach (1957) identified two distinct disciplines of psychology. One comprises areas such as social, developmental, cognitive, physiological and behavioural psychology – branches that try to understand the broad laws that govern how people *in general* behave under various conditions. The second branch is that of individual differences, clinical and (some) occupational psychology, which focuses on how and why people differ from one another. And whilst there have been moves to reconcile these two approaches through experimental designs that consider both types of experimental treatment and individual differences, such studies still remain the exception rather than the rule.

Individual differences

The psychology of individual differences is traditionally divided into four main areas: first, the psychology of motivation (which tries to explain what drives people to behave in certain ways); second, mood/emotion, which considers feelings (one area where there is genuine integration between individual differences and cognitive psychology thanks to workers such as Bower, 1981); third, personality psychology which tries to explain both what people do and the way that they do it through 'personal styles', such as anxiety or sociability. Finally, there is the psychology of abilities, which examines how well individuals perform problem-solving tasks, attempts to understand how many 'talents' are necessary to explain individual differences in problem-solving behaviour and seeks to understand why and how individual differences in these abilities emerge in the first place. Underpinning these four areas is the science of psychometrics (literally 'measurement of the soul'), which is a branch of statistics dealing with the measurement of motivation, mood, personality and abilities, and other issues (e.g. bias) arising from psychological testing.

The psychology of ability is important for several reasons.

• It is interesting in its own right. There are plenty of folk-law stereotypes describing the structure of abilities (e.g. the 'nutty professor' who may be wonderful at nuclear physics but has no 'common sense', whatever that is). Are these correct?

• Our culture places considerable emphasis on individual differences in abilities (e.g. at school, when applying for jobs). If we knew how these abilities develop then we could perhaps develop educational strategies to maximise each child's potential.

• The assessment of abilities is one of psychology's greatest success stories. As will be seen in Chapter 6, ability tests are extremely useful in applied psychology, where they are estimated to have saved firms literally billions of dollars through allowing them to select applicants with the greatest potential for success (Kanfer *et al.*, 1995: 597).

• There is a need for psychology to consider both within-subject factors (individual differences) and between-subject factors (situations, stimuli) to predict how individuals will behave. Psychology will ultimately have to reconcile these two sub-disciplines, as discussed in the following section.

This book focuses on the psychology of **intelligence** and ability, and has three main aims. First of all, it describes what is known about the nature of abilities: in which main ways do people differ from each other, and what causes these individual differences to emerge? Second, it considers some important applications of ability testing, such as personnel selection. Finally, we enter some rather controversial waters, and look at the origins and social consequences of ability. To what extent are our abilities innate, and to what extent are they moulded by our families and schools? And what should we make of recent studies that suggest that social factors are far *less* important than mental abilities when trying to predict which individuals will be unemployed, criminal or single parents?

Cronbach's message

In the previous section we echoed Cronbach's (1957) sentiment that it is necessary to design experiments that take into account both independent variables and individual differences in order to understand or explain behaviour. An example may make this clearer. Suppose that a teacher wants to discover whether the E-numbers in brightly coloured sweets affect children's powers of concentration. She may give one group of children twenty of these sweets each, give each child in a 'control group' twenty sweets with the same calorific value that do not contain any E-numbers, and then measure the performance of both groups on some task that demands concentration, using a t-test or analysis of variance to compare the scores of the two groups. Here the independent variable is the presence or absence of E-numbers in the sweets, and the dependent variable is the task that requires concentration. Table 1.1 shows some hypothetical data from just such an experiment. The first two columns show the extroversion and concentration scores of the nine children in the control group, whilst the final two columns show these data for the eight children in the experimental group. The average concentration scores for the two groups are exactly the same, so a t-test will show no

TABLE 1.1 Hypothetical scores of two groups of children on a task measuring concentration (their extroversion scores are also shown)

No E-numbers		E-numbers	
Extroversion	Concentration	Extroversion	Concentration
10	20	10	13
11	22	11	13
11	18	11	14
12	17	12	19
12	21	12	21
12	23	13	23
13	20	13	26
13	19	14	31
14	20		

significant effect of treatment-type. But the t-test completely fails to identify a hugely significant effect in these data.

The teacher *could* also test to see whether personality (or ability) plays a part in determining the children's responses to E-numbers. On examining the data by eye, it is clear that the E-numbers increase the performance of extroverted (sociable) children but decrease the performance of introverted (quiet) children, whilst having little or no effect on children with moderate levels of extroversion. So although there is no overall shift in mean score (since half the children are introverted whilst half are extroverted), it is clear that the experimental treatment (type of sweet administered) does affect the performance of children: it just does not affect them all in the same way. *This obvious result will be entirely missed by t-tests, analysis of variance and most other standard statistical tests.* There *are* statistical techniques that can reveal what is really going on in experiments like this (one is called 'analysis of covariance'), but unfortunately these are rarely taught to undergraduates (or postgraduates), and so most experimental psychologists continue making the naïve assumption that the people who take part in their experiments are totally identical. So whilst the psychology of individual differences is rather different from the rest of psychology, there is a strong argument for measuring various types of individual differences and incorporating such measures into traditional experimental designs.

The meaning of 'ability'

It is first necessary to try to define the subject-matter of this book: to set out what is meant by terms such as 'mental ability' and 'intelligence'. There is no shortage of definitions in the literature, but many of these are unenlightening: the great and the good from the world of psychology were invited to define what they understood by 'intelligence' at a symposium in 1921 (Thorndike, 1921) and, as usual when psychologists are gathered together, the range of definitions was enormous, running from the rather unhelpful behaviourist view that 'intelligence is what is measured by intelligence tests' to 'ability to learn', or 'capacity for abstract thinking'. Sternberg and Salter (1982) offer a thoughtful historical discussion of what is meant by terms such as 'intelligence', 'mental ability' and 'aptitude', but let us try to build our own definition.

Abilities, in the broad sense, are any behaviours that can sensibly be evaluated. They will include typing, knowledge of steam locomotives, sprinting (and other sporting activities), reading a map, swindling people, cooking, managing one's finances, designing bridges, thinking up a plausible excuse to obtain an extension for a piece of coursework, growing onions, helping a depressed person, solving anagrams, diagnosing a fault in a piece of machinery or writing a creative essay. The key point is that it would be possible to assess the effectiveness of each of these activities, either by:

- monitoring behaviour (e.g. the number of words typed per minute, annual cost of rectifying design faults found in bridges, size/taste/yield of onions, time taken to run 400 metres, success at obtaining extensions), or by

- asking others to evaluate behaviour (e.g. by giving a student a mark for the creative essay or asking depressed individuals to rate the quality of their therapy). Where subjective ratings are used to assess performance it is particularly important to ensure that they are accurate: that is, that the measures have both 'reliability and 'validity'.

Abilities and attainments differ from other areas of individual differences (e.g. the study of mood, motivation or personality) in that it is possible in principle (if not always in practice) to evaluate a person's performance on each of them. For whilst it is possible to measure characteristics such as 'sociability' and 'nervousness' in people, a person with a high score on either of these characteristics is in no sense 'better' than someone with a low score. However, when dealing with abilities it is common practice to assign people numbers indicating their relative levels of performance, either through monitoring behaviour, rating behaviour, or administering psychological tests. Some examples of ability tests and test items are given in Chapters 2 and 6.

Ability tests can be constructed using several different techniques (see for example Cooper, 1998: ch. 18; Kline, 1986). For example, one way of constructing a comprehension test would be to take a dictionary and draw a sample of words (each of which may have only one meaning) from it at random. It would also be necessary to *check* that each word has only one meaning, and that words that are very obscure, very common, very technical or potentially offensive are removed. The correct definition (plus four incorrect ones) of fifty or so of these words could be given to a sample of people, who are asked to identify the one correct definition of each word. The test would generally be scored by giving one point for each correct answer. If the test consists of a large, broad sample of words from the language, then the total scores on this test should accurately reflect the extent of people's verbal comprehension. The test measures what it claims to (it is 'valid') with little measurement error (it is 'reliable'). The beauty of using tests such as these is that they are quick and easy to administer and they do not rely on subjective assessments (as with marking essays).

Mental and other abilities

Readers may feel some unease at this point since the list of abilities given above seems to be far more extensive than one might expect in a psychology text. Surely this book is not going to turn into a treatise on onion-growing? And indeed it is conventional (though not, I believe, necessarily a good thing) to narrow down the field of abilities.

Each of the abilities in the above list can be regarded as reflecting a different mixture of at least four things:

- specific knowledge, attainment or training
- physical prowess
- thought processes
- emotional skills.

For example, typing ability reflects little more than training and practice: one does not have to think about it, and most people in the general population will have the physical ability to use a keyboard. So too is much of the knowledge taught in schools, where a test of 'history attainment' is more likely to measure how well you can remember the content of a particular book rather than anything to do with 'potential'. Much of the individual variations in sporting skills amongst the general population will be related to physical ability and training. Talking to the depressed individual will require some emotional sensitivity (the successful therapist will positively ooze warmth, congruence and unconditional positive regard: Rogers, 1959), as might asking for a coursework extension. However, writing a creative essay, solving anagrams and reading a map are abilities that would seem to largely reflect thought processes, rather than any of the other three types of ability mentioned above, provided that we can assume that anyone who has been through the education system will be able to read and write.

One of the great problems with psychology is that it is often divided up in some rather arbitrary ways. Occupational psychologists and sports psychologists (amongst others) are interested in abilities that have a substantial physical component. Clinical psychology focuses on emotional abilities. Educators and occupational psychologists are interested in the effects of knowledge and training upon performance. And psychologists who are interested in cognitive psychology and individual differences tend to focus their attention on tasks that depend substantially on thought processes for their success. This book follows convention, and focuses on just a small set of abilities – those which require a substantial degree of thought for their successful completion, and which assume no knowledge, physical or emotional skills other than those which everyone can be assumed to have gained as part of their education and development.

Whatever happened to 'intelligence'?

The discussion so far has focused on 'abilities', whereas most of us are more accustomed to use the term 'intelligence' when evaluating individual differences in cognition. I have tried to avoid using the word 'intelligence' in this book, for three reasons. The first is that it may not exist, and using this term essentially prejudges the issues discussed in Chapter 2. For the notion of 'intelligence' generally implies a sort of 'general cognitive aptitude', [1] which suggests that if individuals excel in one area (e.g. memory) they are also likely to excel in others (e.g. spatial skills, the use of language). Whilst this *may* be the case, it seems better to talk more generally in terms of 'abilities', of which 'general ability' or *g* may or may not be one. The second reason is that 'intelligence' seems to have acquired strong links with the classroom through the use of intelligence/ability tests to identify special learning needs. This is probably a bad thing in that it may suggest that 'intelligence' is mainly concerned with knowledge acquisition at school – which it is not (primarily). The third reason is that the terms 'intelligent' or 'high IQ' have become value-laden. In the 1940s, terms such as 'moron', 'idiot' and 'cretin' were

---

[1] The exception being the work of Howard Gardner (discussed in Chapter 3) who speaks of 'multiple intelligences'.

routinely used to describe certain levels of intellectual performance. We may have dropped these terms from polite vocabulary, but the negative overtones associated with low intelligence still linger on. There are plenty of callous monsters with high IQs, as the history books and personal experience testify, and it is all too easy to overvalue the importance of 'intelligence'.

Overview of other chapters

The structure of abilities

There are three main issues that run through research in individual differences. The first is how one should conceptualise (i.e. classify) the subject-matter. We need to understand how many different mental abilities there are, and how they interrelate. This is sometimes known as the 'structural model', as it seeks to describe the basic nature of personality, mood, motivation or abilities. We have already come across one structural model – the term 'intelligence' implies that a person will have a similar level of performance on all abilities. However, one of the main concerns of individual difference psychologists is discovering the most accurate model to describe human abilities. For the number of tasks where individual differences in cognitive performance could be assessed (which is, you will recall, our putative definition of ability) is potentially very large indeed. There has to be some way of grouping these together: to view performance on a number of these tasks as being influenced by a smaller number of basic abilities.

The individual differences literature from the 1920s until the 1970s reports numerous attempts to identify various cognitive tasks that measured the same underlying abilities. Very often a statistical technique known as **factor analysis** was used to help make such decisions. However, technical (and other) problems with this method made the early results seem contradictory. Some researchers claimed that just one ability influenced performance on all tasks; others found evidence for at least a dozen quite different abilities. Thus Chapter 2 of this book explores how factor analysis has been used to reveal the underlying structure of ability, and how there is now fairly good agreement about the underlying structure of abilities.

Chapter 3 considers other structural theories: ways of conceptualising abilities that do not rely on factor analysis. Howard Gardner's (1983, 1993) theory of multiple intelligences draws on a number of sources of evidence (including the effects of brain damage and observation of the way in which different aspects of performance emerge together in developing children) to suggest an alternative to the factor-analytic findings. Interestingly enough, there is substantial overlap between Gardner's work and the models arising from factor analysis, even though they are based on quite different sources of data. Robert Sternberg (1985), on the other hand, uses a very broad definition of ability. He is interested not just in the sorts of cognitive tasks that are traditionally used in intelligence tests (tasks that are deliberately made abstract – decontextualised – so as to minimise the influence of life experiences on their difficulty), but also in 'social intelligence' (the sorts of skills we all use in everyday life when dealing with people) and an 'experiential theory' which explains how we come to draw on previous experiences to perform complex sequences of mental operations smoothly, easily and automatically. The third topic considered in this chapter is, essentially, an anti-theory. Michael Howe (1988b, 1997) has made some interesting points about the whole nature of human abilities, arguing that is utterly wrong to regard abilities as being some properties of the individual that *cause* them to behave in certain ways. At best, Howe says, we can use the term 'abilities' to *describe* how people behave – never to explain it.

Ability processes

A second important topic deals with how and why different people end up showing different types of abilities. What is it that *causes* these individual differences to come about? Could it be something to do with the way the **neurones** in the brain are interconnected

11

or operate? Is there any evidence that abilities have a **genetic** basis? And precisely which cognitive processes are performed when people tackle the items in ability tests? Some of these issues are addressed in Chapters 4 and 5. Chapter 4 examines whether or not genetically similar individuals also have scores on ability tests that are highly similar, or whether it is the way in which children are brought up that determines their eventual levels of ability. This is a highly controversial area, with some workers arguing that there is no evidence that genes play any part in influencing children's cognitive performance, whilst others suggest that up to 70 per cent of the variation of general ability within the population can be explained by genetic influences.

If abilities seem to have a substantial genetic component, then it is logical to try to understand individual differences in ability using biological (rather than social, economic or political) models, since genes directly influence the biological makeup of the nervous system. Chapter 5 thus examines several experiments designed to show whether general ability is linked to the speed and/or efficiency with which nerve cells in the brain transmit information. These vary from simple tasks measuring speed of perception and speed of responding to experiments that seek to determine whether any features of electrical activity recorded from the scalp are related to cognitive ability. We also examine a brave attempt (by Sternberg) to predict how long it takes people to solve fairly complicated tasks, such as **analogies,** by estimating how long it takes them to carry out each of the '**elementary cognitive operations**' involved.

Correlates of ability

There is considerable interest in the extent to which performance on ability tests relates to real-life abilities. If we develop tests to measure the main cognitive abilities, how accurately can we predict how individuals will perform in real-life settings – such as employment? Chapter 6 therefore examines how useful ability tests are for selecting individuals for various occupations – a topic that also has some theoretical importance, as some critics have suggested that the only thing that ability tests can measure is ability at taking ability tests! If test scores can be shown to **correlate** with real-life criteria (such as those related to education or job-performance for example) then this objection can be safely ignored. Much controversy has surrounded an attempt by Herrnstein and Murray (1994) to study whether levels of general ability are reliably linked to important social phenomena – e.g. welfare dependency, crime or the likelihood of bearing a child outside marriage. We also examine these findings in some detail in Chapter 6. Chapter 7 integrates the material from the previous chapters and briefly summarises what is known (and what is *not* yet known) about the psychology of abilities.

Summary

This chapter has introduced some important concepts and terms, and has outlined how the remainder of this book is structured. We examined what is meant by the terms 'individual differences', and 'ability', to draw out the distinction between knowledge or attainment and ability. We digressed to consider Cronbach's plea to integrate the psychology of individual differences with the techniques of experimental psychology when carrying out research, and then considered three important issues in the psychology of abilities: the number/nature/structure of abilities, the reasons why different people have different levels of abilities, and the link between performance on ability tests and behaviour in real life.

Further reading

Barratt, E.S. (1995) 'History of personality and intelligence research', in D. Saklofske and M. Zeidner (eds) *International Handbook of Personality and Intelligence*, New York: Plenum. A brief history of how research in intelligence and personality has developed.

Carroll, J.B. (1997a) 'Psychometrics and public perception', *Intelligence* 24: 25–52. Gives six main propositions about intelligence/abilities that will be developed in subsequent chapters: the discussion of factor analysis will be useful preparation for Chapter 2.

Cronbach, L.J. (1957) 'The two disciplines of scientific psychology', *American Psychologist* 12: 671–684. Argues that in order to predict behaviour it is necessary to consider both 'general laws' of psychology (e.g. learning theory, cognitive psychology) and individual differences (e.g. personality and abilities).

Eysenck, H.J. (1962) *Know your Own IQ*, Harmondsworth: Penguin. Working through this book will demonstrate items measuring general ability and give you useful experience in the practicalities of scoring and interpreting the results from an ability test. It also gives a rough estimate of your own level of general ability. Warmly recommended!

Jensen, A.R. (1998) *The g Factor*, New York: Praeger. Chapter 1 gives another useful summary of the history of research into general ability.

The structure of mental abilities

EVEN THOUGH WE HAVE narrowed the field of study considerably by excluding abilities with a strong physical, emotional
or knowledge-based component, the number of potential mental
abilities is still enormous, and it is not obvious from inspection
which abilities should go together – even in the same domain.
For example, take language. Are adults who can quickly comprehend a written passage also likely to be perform above-average
on tests measuring spelling ability, creative writing, compre-
hending a passage when it is read to them, explaining the meaning
of proverbs, solving anagrams or rapidly thinking of words that
start with the letter 'b' and end with the letter 'n'? In another
domain, are children who can manipulate fractions also able to
solve simultaneous equations, solve geometrical problems and
perform long multiplications without using a calculator or pencil?
It might be the case that some measures of ability (by which we
include performance on tests, behaviours and ratings) tend to rise
and fall together, so that a particular person will tend to have a
similar (high, low or intermediate) score relative to others on all
these measures. Think of the scores on each of the tests as showing
the rank-order of that individual relative to other people in the
school, town, population or world. Indeed, there are three main
possibilities.

First, at one extreme, it might be found that all abilities are
independent. That is, there might be no relationship at all between
how well a particular person can comprehend or remember a
passage, solve anagrams, manipulate fractions, spell, solve simultaneous equations, or carry out any of the other tasks mentioned
above. All of the various abilities might be 'uncorrelated'. So if
one wanted to appraise a person's strengths and weaknesses (as
part of an employer's selection test, for example) it would be
necessary to measure a vast number of different skills. Thus if we
were to plot four individuals' scores on eight different tests

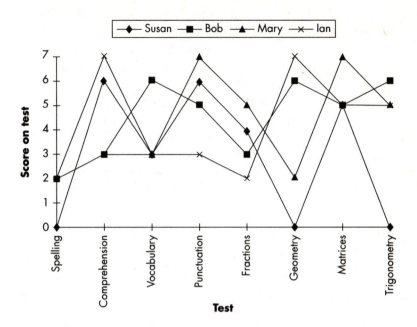

FIGURE 2.1 Scores of four individuals on four tests of verbal skills and four tests of numerical skills, showing no relation between any of the scores

measuring the four verbal skills (V1 to V4) and four numerical skills (N1 to N4) the results would look rather as shown in Figure 2.1.

You will notice that there is little tendency for any person to perform consistently better or worse than others: each person performs well at some tests and poorly at others, and the rank-ordering varies considerably from test to test. Thus, to describe a person's abilities, it is necessary to consider that person's performance on all eight tests.

Second, it might be found that there are some areas of overlap between performance on the various tests. Perhaps people who are below-average on verbal comprehension also perform below-average on all the verbal skills mentioned above, so these form a group of related abilities that 'correlate positively' together.

It might also be found that people who perform above-average on one of the numerical skills also tend to perform well at others, so that these form another group of skills. But it might be found that performance on the numerical tests is unrelated to performance on the verbal tests.

This is shown in Figure 2.2, where each person's level of performance (relative to the other three individuals) on the four verbal tests remains similar: Bob outperforms Mary who outperforms Ian who outperforms Susan on the verbal tests. For the four numerical tasks you can see that there is again some consistency in performance: Ian generally outperforms Bob whilst Susan and Mary both seem to have difficulties with these tests. There

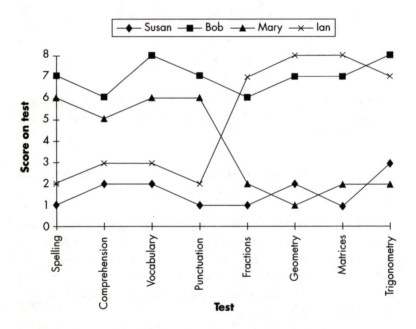

FIGURE 2.2   Scores of four individuals on four tests of verbal skills and four tests of numerical skills, showing that each individual performs to a similar level on all the verbal tests and all the numerical tests but that performance on the verbal test is unrelated to their numerical performance

is some consistency of behaviour within each set of tasks, but little or none *between* the verbal and numerical tasks: a child who is near the top of the class for all of the language problems may well not be near the top of the class for numerical problems. If data show this pattern, it is possible to describe a person's abilities by using just two of the tests (one from the verbal group, and one from the numerical group),[1] rather than the eight previously needed, as there is a lot of overlap between the four verbal tests and between the four numerical tests.

The third possibility is shown in Figure 2.3. This is the simplest model of all: it suggests that a pupil who is near the top

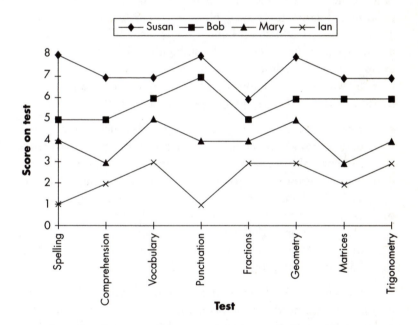

FIGURE 2.3 Scores of four individuals on four tests of verbal skills and four tests of numerical skills, showing that each individual performs to a similar level on all tests

---

[1] Or one test that is a mixture of the four verbal tasks and another that is a mixture of the four numerical tasks.

of the class on one test is also likely to be top of the class on all other tests – no matter whether the other tests are language or numerical in nature. It implies that any one test (or a new test comprising a mixture of items from all eight tests) would be adequate to describe a child's performance.

Factor analysis

Examining graphs such as those in Figures 2.1–2.3 is not the most scientific method of examining the relationships between the children's scores to the various tests. Instead a statistical technique called *factor analysis* is generally used. There are several good introductory texts available (Child, 1990; Comrey and Lee, 1992; Cooper, 1998: chs. 13 and 14; Gorsuch, 1983; Kline, 1994) and Eysenck (1953) remains both highly relevant and easy to grasp. The technicalities of factor analysis need not concern us here: all you need to know is that a computer program reads in the test scores of (100+) people, and indicates:

- whether there are any groups of variables such that a person who scores above-average on one test in the group also tends to score above-average on the others. In Figure 2.2 there are two groups of variables, with just one group in Figure 2.3 and as many groups as there are tests in Figure 2.1.
- which variables belong to each group. For example, in Figure 2.2, the four verbal tests comprise one group, whilst the numerical tests form the other. In Figure 2.3 all the tests belong to one group.

'Groups' are usually termed **factors,** and so we would say that two *factors* are needed to explain the data shown in Figure 2.2, and one factor explains Figure 2.3. The decision about which variables belong to each group ('factor') is made on statistical grounds alone: it is not necessary to 'tell' the program that the first few variables are language-type problems and the remainder are mathematical items. It is quite possible for the factors to be based on different-sized groups, and for some variables (tests) not to appear with *any* of the factors. For example, if we factor analysed ten tests we might find one factor of four tests, another of three tests, and another of two tests – meaning that one of the tests does not belong to any of the factors.

Factor analysis is a very popular technique because it allows one to find groups of items that seem to be measuring the same basic ability. If it is found that the four verbal tests form a factor, this implies that someone who performs well at one verbal problem is likely to perform well on all of them. Someone who performs poorly at one is likely to perform below-average on all the rest, too. This is valuable for four reasons. First, it tells us that it is quite legitimate to construct a test based on a mixture of the four verbal skills – for although the four tests may look rather different, the factor analysis shows that they are all measuring the same underlying ability. The second point is practical: being able to develop tests like this makes the applied psychologist's life much easier, since it means that instead of measuring thousands of different abilities the psychologist need assess only as many abilities as there are factors. Third, it is valuable in helping us understand the structure of ability. Are there any correlations between the numerical ability factor and other factors? Finally, what are the processes that cause a factor to emerge? Why should certain skills form a factor? Do certain children excel at all aspects of mathematics because of the way it has been taught? Or because they carry out certain cognitive processes faster than others? Could it even be related to individual differences in the physiological structure or function of the brain? We shall return to these issues later.

Spearman's *g*

What actually happens when factor analysis is used to explore the relationships between several, seemingly rather different, ability tests? One of the very first studies was performed in 1904 by the British psychologist Charles Spearman, who invented factor analysis for that very purpose. Other workers such as Alfred Binet (in France), Francis Galton (in Britain) and J. McKeen Cattell (in the United States) had previously studied rather simple tasks (e.g. time to perceive pictures, and **reaction time**) and used performance on these tasks to predict success in later life, with rather discouraging results. Spearman's data are interesting for two reasons. First, his work uses somewhat more complex tasks than those chosen by Binet, Galton and Cattell. Second, he was not so much interested in predicting later achievements as in understanding the relationship between several (superficially very different) aspects of ability.

Spearman developed some rather primitive tests, including measures of the children's ability to follow complex instructions, visualisation, vocabulary, mathematical ability, visualisation, ability to match colours accurately and ability to match the pitch of two musical tones. He administered these tests to small samples of children (mainly from a village school in Hampshire), subjected the data to factor analysis and found that a single factor seemed to run through this whole set of tests. A child who scored well above-average on one test also tended to perform well above-average on all the rest. A child who performed at the average level on one of them was unlikely to shine (or obtain a low mark) on any of the others. In other words, Spearman found that the model shown in Figure 2.3 fitted his data rather accurately. He called this factor *general intelligence* (or *general ability*), which is often abbreviated as *g*. Today many psychologists still believe that this 'g-factor' is one of the more useful ways of conceptualising human ability, and the search for the origins and correlates of *g* continues unabated (see for example Jensen, 1998).

One necessary consequence of Spearman's finding is that when several ability tests are correlated together, the correlations between them are invariably positive, a finding that is sometimes called *positive manifold*. Spearman's early work can certainly be criticised on many grounds: the tests that he used may well have been influenced by certain aspects of the children's schooling, his method of factor analysis is now regarded as primitive, mistakes were made in some of his calculations (Fancher, 1985), and his samples were both small (fewer than forty children) and arguably unrepresentative of the broad population of British schoolchildren. Nevertheless Spearman had stumbled on a very broad, powerful effect. We now know that it is impossible to find a half-decent ('reliable' and 'valid' being the technical terms) test that does *not* correlate positively with all other ability tests. As Jensen (1997) observes:

> It [g] is reflected by every cognitive test that permits responses that can be scored or measured according to an objective standard (e.g. number of correct responses, response time) . . . Since its discovery by Spearman in 1904, the g factor has become so firmly established as a major psychological construct in terms of psychometric and factor analytic criteria that further research along these lines is unlikely to disconfirm the construct validity of g or to add anything essentially new to our understanding of it.
>
> (Jensen, 1997: 115 and and 122)

Thurstone's primary mental abilities

Although Jensen's comments reflect mainstream opinion in the 1990s, it was not always thus. In the 1920s and 1930s, Louis Thurstone, in the United States, examined the correlations between certain mental tests in some detail, and reached conclusions that were diametrically opposed to Spearman's. Using a somewhat different method of factor analysis and a wider selection of tests, he found several distinct ability factors rather than g. That is, he found that the model shown in Figure 2.2 fitted the data much better than Spearman's one-factor model (Figure 2.3). When he examined the correlations between fifty-six psychological tests, Thurstone (1938) found not one factor but about a dozen of them, many of which seemed to make good psychological sense. For example, one factor consisted of those tests that involved visualising geometrical figures: such as deciding whether or not the figure shown on the left of Figure 2.4 (lower part) could be rotated to look like the figure shown on the right.

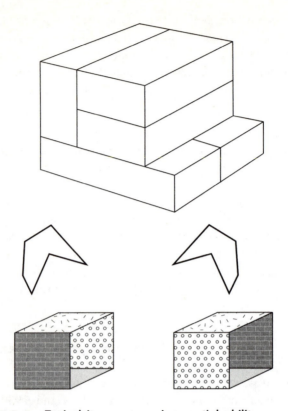

FIGURE 2.4 Typical items measuring spatial ability
Top: How many blocks (each of the same size and shape) are in the top figure?
Middle and bottom: Can the figure on the left be rotated to look like the figure on the right?

Thurstone's other **primary mental abilities** ('PMAs') are shown in Table 2.1, and examples of the actual test items used are reproduced in Chapter 2 of Thurstone (1938).

Thurstone believed that just as the three primary colours of light (red, green and blue) can be combined so as to reproduce any other colour of the spectrum (e.g. yellow), it should be possible to predict a person's performance on any complex cognitive task (e.g. programming a computer, diagnosing electrical faults) through some combination of these PMAs (Thurstone, 1938).

TABLE 2.1 Some of Thurstone's (1938) primary mental abilities, with illustrative examples

Code	Name	Description	Examples
V	Verbal relations	Using words in context	Understanding proverbs, vocabulary, arranging words in order to form a sensible sentence, verbal analogies ('fish is to water as bird is to . . .')
P	Perceptual speed	Speed/accuracy in comparing items or shapes	Are the following two strings of symbols identical? 3%&@^$f\partial$W 3%&@A$f\partial$W
N	Numerical facility	Algebra and other forms of mathematical operation	Solve $y = x^2 - 3x + 3$. What is 40% of 60? Simplify $\dfrac{x^2 - 1}{x - 1}$
W	Word fluency	Tasks dealing with isolated words	Make as many words as you can from the letters A-B-D-E-R. Write down as many words as you can that start with 'A' and end with 'R'. Spelling.
M	Memory	Paired-associate learning and recognition	Pairs of two-digit numbers (e.g., 23 57), words & numbers ('egg 14'), or initials/surname (J.B. Foster) are learnt, and recalled on cue, e.g. 23–?–, –?– 14, –?– Foster.

TABLE 2.1 Contd.

Code	Name	Description	Examples
I	Induction	Finding rules given exemplars	What is the next number in the series 0, 1, 3, 8, 15 ...?
			What do cows, tables and triathlons have in common? (legs)
R	Restriction	A strange mixture of multiple-choice tests	Is 3.1452×7.88814 (a) 24.8098 (b) 17.8848 (c) 21.9098 (d) 30.8848
			A doge is (a) a magistrate (b) a ruse (c) a leaf (d) an idea
D	Deduction	Deductive logic	All tigers are dangerous. Tibbles is dangerous. Is Tibbles a tiger?
S	Spatial ability	Visualising shapes	See, for example, Figure 2.4

Thurstone could find no evidence whatsoever for g. So how could two researchers, both employing similar research techniques (factor analysis) arrive at such different (and seemingly irreconcilable) conclusions? There are several reasons.

- Thurstone tested university students, rather than school-children: this could be important because if students are generally of above-average intelligence, the student group will (by definition) show less variation in g than does the general population. This will tend to lower the correlations between the tests, which will in turn affect the results of the factor analysis, and make it less easy to identify a g factor.

- Thurstone's tests also had strict time limits, whereas Spearman's children were not hurried: it is possible that hurrying students may introduce some random error into the students' scores. I mention this as a possibility: however, research by P.E. Vernon (1961) suggests that this is unlikely to be a problem.

- Thurstone administered a much larger sample of tests than did Spearman (sixty, as opposed to about seven) and the increased size of his sample (200+) can only improve the accuracy of his results.

- As I have observed elsewhere (Cooper, 1998), another crucial difference between Spearman's and Thurstone's experiments lay in the types of tests that were used. Spearman added together scores on addition, subtraction, multiplication problems and so on to estimate the children's overall mathematical ability. He included this *overall* measure of mathematical ability in his factor analyses. Thurstone, on the other hand, treated addition, subtraction, multiplication, etc. as separate tests in his factor analyses. Unsurprisingly, perhaps, his factor analysis revealed that children who did well at addition and subtraction problems also excelled at multiplication and division problems: these four tests formed a factor. So the *factor* of numerical ability identified by Thurstone is almost identical to the *test* of mathematical ability used by Spearman. The problem is not restricted to mathematical ability: Thurstone's collection of tests included some that appeared to be almost identical to other tests in the battery – for example, 'Reading 1' and 'Reading 2' which were two almost-identical tests of knowledge of proverbs. Since these tests are essentially identical, they are virtually *guaranteed* to correlate highly together and form a factor.

How many primary mental abilities are there? This is, in fact, a very difficult question to address, since the choice of sub-tests (and hence the nature of the primary abilities that emerge) is largely arbitrary. Thurstone's (1938) rationale for selecting that particular set of fifty-six tasks was to 'include a fairly wide variety of tests covering verbal, numerical, and visual tasks in the hope that some of the primary traits involved in current psychological tests would appear' (1938: 10). Quite why he concentrated on these three broad areas, and why he chose some tasks rather than others was never made explicit. This is problematical, since if none (or only one)[2] of the tasks in a battery of tests actually measure a particular primary ability, then no factor corresponding to that primary ability can emerge. Thus it is necessary to examine performance on as many diverse tasks as possible. Later studies (e.g. Hakstian and Cattell, 1976) *did* extend the list of tasks used, and discovered more primary abilities as a consequence: the list of primaries now numbers at least twenty, and these take some three hours to assess. However, even this list is unlikely to be complete, as there is always the possibility that some important tasks may have been overlooked.

It certainly *seems* as if there are some major gaps in the sorts of tasks that have been considered. One might perhaps expect the main tasks used to identify the main primary mental abilities to reflect current thinking in cognitive psychology or developmental psychology: it seems reasonable to ensure that a test battery includes those which experimental psychologists use to assess memory for events, Piagetian 'conservation tasks', and so on. However, this is manifestly not the case. Even the classic tasks used by cognitive psychologists (e.g. Clark and Chase, 1972; Posner and Mitchell, 1967; Sternberg, 1969; Stroop, 1935) have generally been ignored in large-scale studies aimed at clarifying the main primary abilities, although Carroll (1983; 1993: 478–509 has scrutinised the factors that emerge when small groups of these tasks are analysed.

Practical considerations (such as the need for quick group testing) may have led to other omissions. For example, there have been few attempts to measure individuals' ability to sing a note in tune, learn a foreign language, track a moving object on a

---

[2] A factor is, by definition, a *group* of tasks that measure the same psychological construct. Thus one task cannot constitute a factor.

computer screen using a joystick, ignore information from one sensory modality when using another (e.g. ignoring words presented through headphones when learning words from a printed list) or measure the speed with which individuals can 'automatise' (that is, learn to perform automatically) novel tasks. There are often good practical reasons for these omissions, but it is likely that the number of potential primary abilities is very large indeed and it is not obvious that we shall ever be able to identify them all. All we can hope to do when assessing abilities for the purpose of personnel selection, clinical diagnosis, the evaluation of educational intervention, or whatever, is to appraise the *main* ability factors.

Individual difference psychologists may have a lesson to learn from occupational psychologists here. It might be worthwhile sampling the sorts of activities that people perform in their working and home lives, and ensuring that any battery of tasks that claims to assess primary mental abilities actually measures all of these variables, in much the same way that occupational psychologists use 'job analysis' to identify the skills required for a particular post. Although the number and nature of the main primary ability factors depends crucially on the nature of the tasks included in the battery, and their 'level' (i.e. sub-tests rather than tests), Kline's (1991) book shows the primary factors identified by Ekstrom *et al.* (1976) and Hakstian and Cattell (1976). Factors that are found in both batteries include perceptual speed (speed of comparing strings such as 1975623097 and 1975643097), numerical ability, spatial ability, verbal comprehension, inductive reasoning, deductive reasoning, memory span (recall of lists of digits), associative memory (memory for 'sensible' phrases – e.g. 'happy sailor'), flexibility of closure (identifying simple figures embedded in more complex ones), speed of closure (identifying words/pictures that have been partially obscured with correcting fluid), word fluency ('list as many words as you can that start with "s" and end in "n"'), originality/flexibility of use of objects ('what object could you make from an empty tin, a stick and a tissue?') and fluency of ideas ('think of as many words as possible that could describe your university/college').

To return to the conflict of views between Spearman and Thurstone, the finding that two researchers who both used factor analysis could come to such different conclusions about the structure of abilities made many psychologists wary of the technique. The debate was intense, as indicated by Thurstone's claim that 'we have not found the general factor of Spearman, but our methods do not preclude it' (Thurstone, 1938: vii). It suggested (to non-specialists) that factor analysis was a flawed procedure that was capable of 'proving' anything – a notion that endures today. For example, Howe (1997: 28) asserts that 'it [factor analysis] does not identify any one unique correct solution', a claim which most would regard as being factually incorrect. But how can one resolve the problem that one researcher identifies a general factor of ability, whilst another finds at least ten? One solution to this conundrum is outlined in the next section.

Hierarchical models of ability

Several researchers (Carroll, 1993; Cattell, 1971; Gustafsson, 1981; Horn and Cattell, 1966; Vernon, 1950) have shown that there is no necessary conflict between the views of Spearman and Thurstone, and that both these models can be viewed as correct when considered as part of a hierarchical model of abilities. It all hinges on the realisation that the *factors* identified by Thurstone (numerical facility, verbal relations, spatial ability, etc.) might themselves be correlated. So it is entirely possible to apply factor analysis to the correlations between these *factors*.

In principle it is a simple matter to follow the steps outlined below, which will reveal the structure of ability.

(a) Devise tests to measure a very large number of rather 'low-level' mental abilities: for example, tests assessing ability to solve anagrams, knowledge of proverbs, ability to multiply two-digit numbers, ability to identify the aesthetically most pleasing picture from a series, ability to remember lists of numbers presented verbally. The key requirement here is that each sub-test should comprise a number of similar items: there should be no attempt to mix items (e.g vocabulary, spelling and comprehension items) within a test, since the *assumption* that these various skills are related is precisely the one that we wish to test. In practice, modern researchers may study the relationship between fifty or more such sub-tests.

(b)   Administer these to large samples of volunteers.

(c)   Work out the scores (number of items correctly answered) for each person on each test.

(d)   Use a computer program to factor analyse these scores: that is, to determine

- how many factors (groups of tests) are present
- which tests belong to which factor(s). The 'primary mental abilities' that emerge at this stage (verbal ability, etc.) are sometimes known as 'first-order factors', as they are found at this, first, step of the analysis.

(e)   Repeat step (d) several more times, but instead of factoring the sub-test scores we now factor the first-order factors (PMAs) to produce **second-order factors** (sometimes known as 'second-order abilities' or 'secondaries', then third-order factors. Thus, we first group the sub-tests to form first-order factors. Then we try grouping these factors to form second-order factors, and so on – until it is found that none of the factors can sensibly be grouped with any other factors, or until just one factor remains.

The answer to the question 'how many ability factors are there?' thus depends entirely on the level of analysis that one wishes to describe. To describe a person's abilities in most detail one would want to measure all known primary factors, which would take many hours. The hierarchical model shows that it is possible to get a very good approximation to this figure by measuring second-order abilities (or primaries that are very closely correlated with the second-order abilities). Or one can get a very reasonable approximation by simply measuring general ability, *g*. Which level of the hierarchy is used depends on the purpose of testing: in particular whether the aim is to predict performance on just a few, highly specific tasks (such as those involved in clerical work, where tests measuring a few primaries such as perceptual speed, verbal and numerical ability are the obvious choice) or to try to predict how a person will perform in a great many (unspecified) areas using a test of *g*.

Horn and Cattell (1966), Hakstian and Cattell (1978), Undheim (1981) and Gustafsson (1981) are amongst those who have used this approach to discover the structure of abilities, although some workers start from the level of primary abilities, rather than the lower-level sub-tests. That is, they use scores on commercially published tests measuring primary mental abilities, such as the Comprehensive Ability Battery (Hakstian and Cattell, 1976), the Kit of Cognitively Referenced Tests (Ekstrom *et al.*, 1976) or the Differential Aptitude Test (Bennett *et al., 1978)* rather than rediscovering the primary mental abilities as described in step (a) above.

The choice of which variables are entered into the analysis is therefore somewhat arbitrary, and will often be based on those primary abilities that happen to be easily assessed by commercial tests. This will itself influence which secondary abilities are found, and there is always the chance that including a few new tasks will produce additional primary and higher-order abilities.

An example may help. Suppose that we took a selection of tests similar to those used by Thurstone, administered them to a large sample of people, calculated the correlations between every pair of tests, and used factor analysis to identify the factors. We might represent the analysis graphically as shown in Figure 2.5. This shows the left-hand portion of a very wide diagram, where the squares to the bottom of this figure each represent some psychological tests, such as those used by Thurstone. So T1 might represent a test measuring understanding of proverbs (e.g 'a bird in the hand is worth two in the bush'), T2 a test of verbal analogies (a typical item being 'cat is to kitten as dog is to . . .'), T3 vocabulary (e.g 'which word in the following list means the opposite of "tiny"'), T4 a measure of comprehension (e.g. asking someone to read a piece of text and then asking questions to test the person's understanding of what has been read), T5 a test asking what certain groups of things have in common, that other objects do not (e.g 'legs' in the case of tables and people, as opposed to snakes, fish and cars), T6 a test asking subjects to complete a difficult number series (e.g. 1, 4, 13, 40), T7 a test of verbal analogies (e.g. 'petrol is to car as ? is to computer') and T8 might ask people to pick a shape that will best complete a pattern. T9 measures memory span (ability to recall lists of numbers read aloud.

You will remember that factor analysis is a statistical procedure that can show which (if any) of the tests measure the same underlying ability as other tests. The ovals represent the *factors* ('primary mental abilities') and a line joining a test to a factor indicates that this particular test 'belongs to' the factor. So in the figure we can see that T1, T2, T3 and T4 all measure one factor, whereas T5–T8 measure a second factor. As it is clear from the nature of the problems in the tests that T1–T5 all involve the use of language, we would probably call the first factor 'verbal ability'

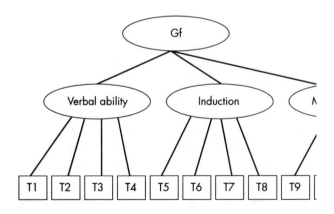

FIGURE 2.5 Part of a hierarchical model of ability, showing how primary mental abilities (verbal ability, inductive reasoning . . .) emerge from the factor analysis of sub-tests, and how a second-order ability factor (fluid ability, Gf) emerges from a factor analysis of the primary mental abilities

or something similar. Likewise it seems from their content that T5–T8 all involve inductive reasoning.

Where this model differs from Thurstone's is that we assume that the factors themselves may be correlated. (Thurstone's method of factor analysis forced the factors to be uncorrelated with each other, purely because it made the analysis easier to perform.) But if we remove this restriction, then it is possible to examine the relationship between the various *factors*, in exactly the same way that we earlier looked at the relationship between the *tests*. It might be found empirically that some factors (including the 'verbal ability' and 'inductive reasoning' PMAs) are correlated together and form a factor denoted here as Gf, whilst other PMAs (such as 'digit span' or 'original uses') form other factors. These factors are known as 'second-order abilities' or 'secondaries'. Likewise there is nothing to stop us exploring the relationships between the secondaries, perhaps finding one or more 'third-order' or 'tertiary' factors. Indeed, the process can continue either until all the factors are uncorrelated, or until just one factor remains.

Gustafsson (1981) studied the relationships between scores on some twenty tasks. These were found to form ten primary mental ability factors, which were themselves found to be inter-correlated. This meant that it was legitimate to look for second-order factors, and Gustaffson found three main second-order factors (all of which had previously been identified by other workers using different selections of tests: e.g. Hakstian and Cattell, 1978; Horn and Cattell, 1966). Fluid intelligence (Gf) was a factor that grouped together the primaries such as inductive and deductive reasoning, memory and ability to make logical infer-ences. Crystallised intelligence (Gc) bundled together primary abilities such as verbal ability, numerical ability and mechanical knowledge/reasoning, primaries that involve both knowledge and abstract thought. Visualisation (Gv) encompassed those primaries that involved 'picturing' what figures would look like if they were moved. These three second-order factors were found to be corre-lated, and so it was appropriate to look for a third-order factor. This factor grouped together all three of the second-order factors. Thus Gustaffson's hierarchical model resembles that shown in Figure 2.5. As before, the ellipses represent factors and the squares represent tests. (To keep the diagram to a manageable size, we have not shown all of the twenty tests, or all ten primary mental abilities.) Straight lines indicate which tests (or factors) fall into groups, as shown in Figure 2.2.

Carroll (1993) used factor analysis to re-examine 461 sets of data, in order to determine which are the most reliably found primary factors. His 800-page discussion is well worth consulting, but in essence he suggests that the main primary abilities include:

- three types of reasoning ability (inductive, deductive and that used in solving mathematical problems)
- five memory factors (memory span and associative memory as discussed above, plus visual memory, memory for meaningful material e.g. 'happy sailor', and free recall memory), together with one 'speed of learning' factor
- between five and eight visual perception factors, including perceptual speed, spatial ability, speed of closure, flexibility of closure (all described above) and visualisation
- twelve auditory factors, including ability to hear faint sounds, to localise sounds in space, understand distorted speech and remember tunes
- nine factors tapping the speed with which ideas can be generated or expressed, including ideational fluency and word fluency
- a great many factors associated with language use
- several factors associated with school achievement/knowledge, and social skills
- speed of speaking, and speed of writing

When tests measuring some of these primary abilities are administered to large groups of people, and the correlations between these tests are factor analysed, the main second-order factors that emerge include those identified by Gustafsson (1981) and described above, namely fluid intelligence (Gf), crystallised intelligence (Gc) and visualisation (Gv). Carroll's analyses also include second-order factors of memory ability (Gm), cognitive speed (Gs) and retrieval (Gr) identified by Cattell (1971), the latter having large loadings from tests such as 'word fluency' or 'originality' requiring information to be retrieved quickly from long-term memory. Carroll's list also includes a factor of auditory perception, plus a rather strange factor that is a mixture of Gc and Gf. When the correlations between these second-order factors are analysed, a factor of general intelligence (g) is found at the third level.

It should now be clear how this model – Carroll (1993) calls it the 'three stratum model' – reconciles the work of Spearman and Thurstone. The model shows that it is perfectly reasonable to describe the correlations between the tests either in terms of rather a lot of primary mental abilities (the first-order factors), or in terms of a few second-order factors, or in terms of general ability (the third-order factor). It is a matter of convenience which level of analysis one chooses.

A concrete example may make this clearer. Suppose that, instead of asking people to carry out cognitive tasks, you asked them to rate (on a seven-point scale) how much they enjoyed certain films. The list of films would be a long one, and should cover the whole spectrum, just as a great many varied tasks are administered when researching the structure of abilities. It would be easy to factor analyse people's responses to the various films using a standard statistics package. Remember that factor analysis will try to identify variables that individuals like to a similar extent, and so one would probably find that *Gunfight at the OK Corral* and *The Magnificent Seven* formed one factor (which we might call 'Westerns'), *Reservoir Dogs* and *Pulp Fiction* formed second ('Urban Reality' films), *Alien* and one of the *Star Trek* films, a third (Science Fiction) factor, *When Harry Met Sally* and *Pretty Woman*, a fourth ('Romantic?') factor, *Police Academy* and *The Full Monty*, a fifth ('Comedy') factor and *A Nightmare on Elm Street* and *Friday the 13th* a sixth ('Horror') primary factor. We could then factor the correlations between these six primary factors and might well find three secondary factors. I would guess that the first of these factors would comprise the Science Fiction and Horror factors, and so might be labelled 'fantasy films', the second secondary factor might include 'Romantic' and 'Comedy' films (perhaps called 'relaxing films') and the final factor might show that the Westerns and Urban Reality films also went together ('violent films'). And finally we might factor the correlations between these three second-order factors and obtain a single, general, factor.

Consider now how you might explain why a particular person likes any particular film – *Alien*, for example. At the narrowest level of generalisation (first-order factor) you could 'explain' it by pointing out that people tend to like science fiction films to a certain, characteristic extent, and this is why the individual enjoys *Alien*. Or we could move up a level, and note that the factor analysis reveals that some people enjoy fantasy films (of which science fiction is one example) whilst others do not, and *this* is why *Alien* appeals. Hence the person may enjoy Alien because it is a fantasy film. Or we could explain it by resorting to the third-order factor, which reveals that some people like *all sorts* of films (of which fantasy films are one example) whilst others are not keen on any sort of film: our viewers might enjoy *Alien* just because they enjoy *all* films. But all three explanations are correct, and useful in trying to explain why an individual may enjoy the film. Which level of explanation we use ('because the person likes films', 'because they like fantasy films' or 'because they like science fiction films') is entirely up to us. Suppose that we wanted to predict how the *Alien* fan would enjoy *Friday 13th*. We might find it useful to make the prediction on the basis of their liking for 'fantasy films', as both science fiction and horror films fall into that category. If we wanted to predict whether they would enjoy *The Full Monty* it would be sensible to consider their liking for films *in general*, since only this will filter down to these two particular films.

It is exactly the same when analysing the structure of abilities. One can 'explain' a person's performance on a particular psychological test either in terms of a primary mental ability (as did Thurstone), in terms of a second-order ability factor (e.g Gf, Gc, Gv, Gr or Gm) or in terms of their general ability, g (as suggested by Spearman).

Summary

This chapter has introduced the method of factor analysis – a valuable tool that can identify which (if any!) of several test scores tend to vary together from person to person. Although Spearman and Thurstone both used factor analysis to explore the structure of abilities, they came to very different conclusions (one factor of 'general ability', g, versus a dozen 'primary mental abilities'). We suggest some reasons for this confusion, and note how both these 'explanations' for the structure of abilities can be correct when viewed within the context of a hierarchical model that includes second- and third-order factors. The best-established primary and second-order ability factors are described.

Further reading

Brody, N. (1992) *Intelligence* (2nd edn), London: Academic Press. Chapters 1 and 2 offer an excellent account of how our knowledge of the structure of abilities has developed.

Carroll, J.B. (1982) 'The measurement of intelligence' in R.J. Sternberg (ed.) *Handbook of Human Intelligence*, Cambridge: Cambridge University Press. A historical overview with some emphasis on how ability tests came to be developed and used.

Child, D. (1990) *The Essentials of Factor Analysis*, London: Cassell. The easiest introduction to the topic for those who want to understand it in more depth.

Eysenck. H.J. (1953) 'The logical basis of factor analysis', *American Psychologist* 8: 105–114. Useful, non-technical description of this important topic.

Jensen, A.R. (1998) *The g Factor*, New York: Praeger. Chapters 1–4 give a clear account of how factor analysis has been used to clarify the structure of abilities: it requires a little more mathematical sophistication than the other references, but anyone who understands the basics of correlations should have no difficulties.

Kline, P. (1991) *Intelligence: The Psychometric View*, London: Routledge. Chapter 3 outlines what is known about the structure of abilities.

Alternative views of the structure of ability

WHILST CHAPTER 2 FOCUSED on attempts to use factor analysis to understand the number of distinct abilities and the interrelations between them, not all theorists have followed this route. For there are some phenomena (such as 'streetwise' intelligence) that the models of ability described in Chapter 2 were not designed to explain, and I believe that the definition should be broadened in order to do so.

The factor-analytic models discussed previously sought to describe how well 'normal' individuals perform. There is a literature (summarised by Howe, 1989) indicating that individuals with severe learning difficulties may nevertheless be capable of exceptionally good cognitive performance in some highly specific areas. For example, Howe cites case histories of individuals whose scores on tests of general ability placed them in the lowest few per cent of the population, but who could nevertheless perform prodigious feats of memory (e.g. memorising chunks of a telephone directory), playing, recognising and identifying music, and performing complex calculations with dates (e.g. being able to work out on which day of the week 3 January 1893 fell). Such data are certainly difficult to reconcile with the models described in Chapter 2.

An additional problem with the analyses described in Chapter 2 is that they do not automatically suggest 'process models' of ability. That is, they do not explain how or why certain children develop certain levels and patterns of ability, whilst others develop rather different skills. Some process models have been proposed (see, for example, Chapters 4 and 5) but these are essentially derived from the hierarchical model described in Chapter 2, and are not an integral part of it. If the process models described in Chapters 4 and 5 could be shown to be completely incorrect, this would not falsify the hierarchical model described in Chapter 2.

A second concern focuses on the nature of the problems typically posed in ability tests. These are frequently (though not always) abstract, and focus on logical 'convergent' problem-solving skills – for example, identifying what characteristic two shapes have in common, and checking to see whether another pair of shapes obeys the same rule. But hardly anyone performs such rarefied tasks in their day-to-day life! A driver may have to work out the fastest route across town when the usual road is blocked by an accident. A salesperson may have to assess how much profit will have to be sacrificed as a discount in order to clinch a sale of a car. A teacher must decide how best to deal with a persistently disruptive student. There are certainly 'intelligent' and 'unintelligent' responses that can be made when one's partner is angry and upset following a forgotten birthday, or when one is unhappy at work and eager to move on. Students arguably show 'intelligence' in the way that they research material for an essay – identifying relevant information from journals, reference books, the Internet, etc. – and then assemble it to form a coherent story. Perhaps ability should be defined in terms of an individual's skills at seeking out and sifting information, and should consider social skills, the ability to modify one's environment, and other rather complex skills? Ceci (1996: ch. 6) cites literature suggesting that children who learn skills in one context (e.g. in a mathematics classroom) have difficulty performing the same operations in a different context. So is it sensible to expect skills shown in the context of ability tests to predict real-life behaviour?

Finally, Howe argues that it is simply inappropriate to regard general ability as an 'explanation' for any sort of behaviour. Even if the sorts of models described in Chapter 2 are found to fit the data rather well, Howe believes that g and all of the other ability factors discussed previously are simply convenient descriptions of how people behave: they should never be used to *explain* the behaviour, as this is 'circular'. For example, suppose that children take a test assessing their ability to solve certain arithmetic problems. It is quite legitimate to conclude from this that a child has a certain level of arithmetic ability. However, it is clearly *not* sensible to then assert that the reason why the child performs well at these problems is because he or she has high arithmetic ability. In this circular definition, a concept (arithmetic ability, *g* or whatever) is used to describe a certain set of behaviours – and also to *explain* why they arise.

This chapter considers three different theories of ability – those of Robert Sternberg, Howard Gardner and Michael Howe. Their theories are very different from each other, but all voice criticisms of the factor-analytic model of abilities discussed in Chapter 2.

Sternberg's triarchic theory of ability

Robert Sternberg's (1985) *triarchic theory* is so named because it seeks to explain how three different types of intelligence operate.

(a) The **componential sub-theory** tries to model how people solve problems. It seeks to explain how we conceptualise problems, plan how to solve them, select strategies or short-cuts, monitor the success of our efforts (and perhaps modify the approach being used) and perform the basic mental operations necessary to reach a solution.

(b) The **contextual sub-theory** examines how individuals adapt their environments, adapt *to* their environments, and select their environments in an 'intelligent' manner.

(c) The **experiential sub-theory** considers the role of past experiences in problem-solving – such as the development of automaticity, where complex sequences of cognitive operations can, after practice, be performed swiftly, smoothly, accurately and almost without thought. Moving a character around the screen when playing a computer game or multiplying single-digit numbers are two obvious examples. This sub-theory essentially tries to explain how individuals try to relate novel events to previous experience or skills.

The componential sub-theory

A 'component' is defined by Sternberg (1985: 97) as 'an elementary information process that operates upon internal representations of objects' – a thought process, in other words. And whilst some of these components are very broad (e.g. thinking in a vague sort of way that you really *ought* to think about preparing for that essay), others may involve rather precise descriptions of cognitive behaviour (e.g. deciding whether two words or shapes are identical). It is not at all obvious which level of generality is the most appropriate: gross generalisations, or minute descriptions that might even operate at the level of firing in individual neurones.

This part of the theory thus considers cognitive operations that range from high-level planning components (*metacomponents*) down to the myriad of low-level cognitive operations (e.g. encoding strategies) that actually get the problem solved. Thus there are three types of components: performance components, metacomponents and knowledge acquisition components.

Performance components

These are the basic 'building blocks' of problem-solving and include many of the cognitive operations (e.g. encoding and retrieving material from memory, mental rotation) that are required in order to perform a task. If one was to draw up a 'flowchart' showing the sequence of operations that a person performs in order to solve some puzzle, the boxes in the flowchart would be the performance component. Sternberg identifies three types of performance components. These include various *encoding components* (noticing what stimuli look like), *comparison components* (deciding whether two stimuli follow some rule, e.g. are the same colour or shape) and *response components* (doing something, e.g. deciding to push one button rather than another).

Sternberg's first experimental studies into performance components began with an approach known as **componential analysis** (Sternberg, 1977). This was a brave attempt to understand the cognitive processes that took place as people solved individual items in ability tests. For example, suppose that a person is shown two words on a computer screen and asked to push one button if they mean the same thing, or another button if they differ in meaning. What mental operations must a person perform in order to make this decision? One simple model might suppose that a person will have to

(a)   read the first word
(b)   retrieve its meaning from some internal 'dictionary' (the time taken to do so being known to depend on features of the word such as its frequency or length) and store this meaning in working memory
(c and d) do the same for the other word
(e)   evaluate whether the two words are 'sufficiently' similar
(f)   make the appropriate response (e.g. by pressing one of two buttons).

Thus an individual's reaction time to this item is a simple sum of the durations of all of these cognitive processes. It is possible that each of the stages listed above (sometimes called *elementary cognitive operations* or ECOs) takes a fixed amount of time for a particular individual. For example, it may take me 0.05 seconds to retrieve words of a particular length and frequency, whilst another individual may be able to perform this operation in 0.03 seconds. Using some ingenious methodologies, Sternberg was able to estimate the durations of several such ECOs. (We will see in Chapter 5 that Sternberg used a rather different task from that shown above – one that did not require the use of language.)

To see why this work is important, suppose that we have estimated the duration of one person's ECOs from one task, and know the nature and sequence in which some of these operations are performed in *another* task. We should be able to 'plug in' the durations of the ECOs and predict quite accurately how long it will take the individual to perform the second task. Unfortunately, however, there is so much measurement error associated with the estimated duration of the ECOs (and/or in deciding which model is the most appropriate) that this is not possible in practice (e.g. May *et al., 1987*).

It turns out that even for simple tasks, the number of potential cognitive models becomes very large. This is because some operations may perhaps be performed in parallel, rather than sequentially. This makes it much harder to work out which model is the 'best', and to estimate the durations of the ECOs. However, the basic idea from this research is that *cognitive components* may affect performance on ability-test items.

Metacomponents

Metacomponents are involved in planning how to solve problems. Consider solving a jigsaw puzzle. One might first decide on a sequence of strategies to use, such as

(a)   sorting the pieces that have a straight edge into several piles, according to their colour
(b)   consulting the picture to decide which coloured pieces of border go where
(c)   assembling chunks of same-coloured border by searching for those that have appropriately shaped contours and testing whether they fit
(d)   joining these sections of border together
(e)   repeating steps (a)–(d) for similarly coloured/textured areas within the main body of the puzzle until it is ultimately solved.

Sternberg suggests that metacomponents are used to:

●   *decide precisely what the problem is that needs to be solved.* This is obvious in the case of the jigsaw, but may not be immediately clear to an arbitrator who is involved in a long-standing, complex and emotional dispute between an employer and a union, or to students who are keen to find a boy or girlfriend but do not know what, precisely, they are doing wrong. This may also affect performance on some well-known cognitive tasks. In my student days I once took part in an experiment on 'conservation of volume', was shown a lump of plasticine and was asked whether it would always displace the same amount of water when dropped into a tank. I said that it would not, arguing to myself that a dense plasticine ball *could* be made to have a hollow, air-filled pocket in the centre. Because I approached the task as one of extreme logical reasoning, I failed to show 'conservation of volume'.

- *select appropriate performance components* in order to solve the problem. There are usually several ways of solving each problem; should one approach the jigsaw by simply trying to randomly fit pieces together?
- *decide how to represent information.* For example, consider whether a diagram might help when solving an abstract reasoning task, such as an anagram.
- *decide how to combine lower-level components.* For example, consider whether to sort for colour, texture and a straight edge simultaneously, or in three stages, and how to decide that a particular chunk of the puzzle seems to be wrong.
- *decide how much time to allocate to each component.* Should each component be performed slowly but accurately, or is it better to aim for quick and possibly faulty analyses?
- *monitor the success* of the solution. That is, check how one's solution is progressing according to the initial plan.
- *incorporate feedback.* Be alert for improved ways to solve the problem that are noticed by chance.

Taken together, the metacomponents describe how a particular problem is to be conceptualised, and which methods (procedures, strategies) may allow its successful solution. For example, suppose that you need to get to a distant village by lunchtime tomorrow. Using the metacomponents described above, you may:

- decide what problems need to be solved (air, rail, coach and local bus timetables, and your bank balance),
- decide to draw a diagram showing how long it will take to get close to the village by rail, air and coach and to make connecting journey by bus or taxi

- decide how best to estimate the earliest time that you will be able to arrive there by all these routes (e.g. telephoning, using the Internet)
- decide how to weigh speed of travel against cost
- decide how accurate you want the estimates of journey time to be
- check that there *is* a solution that will get you there by lunchtime (if not, you may need some other ideas, such as hiring a car)
- perhaps notice that as the airport, train station and coach station are equidistant from the village, it will take the same amount of time to get there by taxi from any of these points, so making it unnecessary to worry about the journey times for the final leg of the trip.

Thus Sternberg's metacomponents essentially describe how we go about conceptualising and solving complex problems.

Knowledge acquisition components

Sometimes people may be aware that an intermediate step in problem-solving ought to be possible, but that they do not have the necessary knowledge or skills to carry it out. For example, when researching an essay, you will flick through books, journals and abstracts until you find something that looks relevant (*selective encoding*), then when reading the full book or paper you will focus on those parts that seem most relevant to your essay, and hook these together. This is known as *selective combination*. Then you may want to link your new-found knowledge to other, related concepts with which you are familiar (*selective comparison*).

General properties of performance components, metacomponents and knowledge acquisition components

Each component is assumed to have three characteristics.

- duration (how long it takes to perform)

- difficulty (the chances that the component will produce the wrong answer)
- probability of execution when solving a particular problem.

For example, the process that compares the colours of two objects is likely to be quick to execute; might give the wrong answer on 10 per cent of occasions (particularly if one is colour-blind or the lighting is poor) and likely to be executed very often when solving the jigsaw puzzle. The cognitive process that finds the larger of two numbers is likely to be slower, may rarely give the wrong answer, and will seldom or never be used when solving a jigsaw puzzle. Individuals are almost *bound* to consider how to solve the jigsaw puzzle most efficiently (a metacomponent) – but even if they muse for hours, they may overlook an obvious strategy.

However; these components are problematical for two reasons. First, as Kline (1991: 117–123) discusses in some detail, many of them are 'non-contingent' concepts. That is, they are concepts whose existence is necessarily implied by the problem. For example, it is clearly impossible to solve any problem without 'encoding' it (making some representation of it). So there must, by definition, be an 'encoding' performance component. Likewise when solving a problem there *has* to be some sort of 'response component' (even if it only involves saying 'aha!' to oneself). Surely 'problem-solving' is by *definition* using metacomponents to decide how to represent the problem, devise strategies for solving it, and so on. And is it possible to learn anything *without* using selective-encoding/combination/comparison? It is not at all obvious that this part of the theory is scientific, in the sense that it cannot obviously be falsified.

Second, the broad definitions of 'components' given above mean that it is impossible to specify the level at which behaviour should be analysed. Take one of the very simplest 'performance components' – pushing a button when a light comes on. One could simply measure the duration/probability of execution/ success of execution of this button-pressing component (using some form of chronometric experiment to estimate the duration of encoding and comparison components, and subtracting these from the total reaction time). Or one can go down to a lower level of analysis, look at what is happening in the neurones and regard *this* activity as a (more complex) set of response components. Having mastered that, we could even try to conceptualise what goes on at a biochemical level. Or take the 'encoding' component. Is this really a single process, or is it possible (necessary, even) to explain encoding in terms of other lower-level sub-processes? As each component may possibly spawn many simpler sub-processes (for 'no claim is made that any of the components are elementary at all levels of analysis': Sternberg, 1985: 98) the types of models used to describe even simple behaviours can rapidly become very, very complex and impossible to test.

The contextual sub-theory

Sternberg argues that it is impossible to identify 'intelligent' behaviour without considering the context in which it takes place. A behaviour such as running which is intelligent in one situation (being chased by a bull) may not be intelligent in another (being chased by a New York police officer). So the contextual sub-theory attempts to understand the interaction between behaviours and the environment. There are three basic ways in which the interaction between a person and an environment may be altered. Individuals may seek to modify the environment, adapt their behaviour to suit the environment, or select a new environment. For example, suppose that one's room is too cold in winter, which makes late-night studying difficult. The options that are available include modifying the environment (obtaining a heater), adapting to the environment (obtaining warm clothes) or selecting a different environment (moving house). Similarly, if one is unhappy with the university course that one has chosen, the options include adapting to it (trying to develop an interest or reminding oneself that one has to study the subject for only another eighteen months), modifying it (by making constructive suggestions for change) or selecting a different environment (by changing course or institution).

This theory sounds intuitively sensible, but may be fraught with problems. For how else *can* one interact with one's environment other than by adapting oneself, modifying the environment or changing the environment? Once again, these seem to be necessary ('non-contingent') concepts, implying that the theory cannot be falsified.

This definition of 'intelligence' also means that a great number of other factors, psychological, social and experiential, will together determine what is the most 'intelligent' option for an individual. They will include:

- the nature of subjects studied prior to university, university regulations and academic practices which may constrain the possibilities that are open to an individual
- motivation
- personality (e.g. self-confidence)
- the structure of an individual's social networks
- social construction processes
- expectations about the consequences of changing course, and so on.

The list is potentially very long indeed. This means that the evaluation of whether or not a person has made an 'intelligent' response to environmental demands has to be made using different criteria for each individual: changing course may be eminently sensible for one person, but not for another. So assessing whether a particular behaviour is 'intelligent' in a particular environmental context is a remarkably complex procedure. Sternberg may have accidentally redefined 'intelligence' to mean 'any form of individual difference or life experience'.

Traditional ability tests have been deliberately decontextualised in order to minimise the effects of all of these variables. The items are generally abstract (involving geometric figures rather dealing with the shapes of fields). The roles of prior experience, motivation, personality, etc. are minimised through the use of instructions, practice items and sensitive administration procedures precisely because it would be very difficult to assess all of these variables and allow for their influence in test-performance.

So which behaviours do most people *regard* as being 'intelligent' in real-life settings? To test this, several writers have studied lay-theories of ability, by assuming that groups of people sampled from the street share the same social context – which seems to be a very major assumption. In the previous paragraphs we have suggested that 'context' is a very personal thing, which may not be at all obvious to others. For example, two people showing the same behaviour (playing golf) may be doing so for two different reasons (playing for pleasure or clinching a business deal); whilst it is perfectly intelligent for the former player to try to win by all legal means, if the second individual is 'intelligent' he or she will let the *client* win. So averaging across people to derive a consensus view seems to make little sense if each person has a different understanding of the 'context' in which they live or behave. However, when people's definitions of 'intelligent behaviour' are averaged, they resemble those definitions used by psychologists (speed of reasoning, problem-solving and social competence: Sternberg, 1985: 63)

A more promising approach involves presenting people with an outline of a plausible real-life problem, the setting of which is familiar (e.g. feeling unhappy with one's course at university) together with some alternative strategies for dealing with it (Sternberg and Wagner, 1986). These authors believe that it is the ability to acquire and use 'tacit knowledge' (knowledge learnt through experience rather than being explicitly taught – e.g. as a result of observing others' experience) that enables people to identify the most 'intelligent' alternative. However this approach, too, fails to consider the unique blend of attitudes, beliefs and values that each individual may being to the situation. So even this may not be a perfect test of the theory.

It is difficult to test whether the contextual sub-theory of intelligence is correct as it is very hard to understand the precise context in which another individual operates. Motivation, values, background, personality, etc. will all constrain the options that are available to the individual, and influence the perceived merits of various courses of action. So it is not at all obvious how one can ever evaluate how 'intelligent' an individual's behaviour really

51

is in a particular situation, since the 'situation' is unlikely ever to be completely understood by someone else.

There is certainly good experimental evidence that suggests that the context in which problems are presented affects their difficulty: studies such as Carragher *et al.* (1985) show that children may find it difficult to apply mathematical skills learnt in a classroom to behaviour in the real world, whilst the converse is also true. That is, the novelty of the situation may influence a person's ability to reason.

The prime advantage of traditional ability tests is that they present people with tasks with which they have had no previous experience. Provided that they have a few basic cognitive capabilities (perhaps just the ability to understand the test instructions and use the answer sheet appropriately) the test should measure their ability to perform a particular sequence of mental operations – e.g. solving anagrams, remembering digits or visualising what geometrical shapes would look like if they were rotated. As soon as one starts to look at real-life capabilities (such as placating a furious boy/girlfriend), a host of other variables may influence performance – prior experience in similar situations, education (both formally, in school, and informally from one's peers and family), personality and mood, the social setting, as well as abilities such as empathy, the ability quickly to consider a wide range of courses of action and choose the most appropriate one, and the ability to express oneself. So defining abilities in this way seems to result in the term 'ability' being stretched to its limit, and made to encompass a huge range of social and psychological phenomena.

The experiential sub-theory

This aspect of the triarchic theory considers the role of experience in problem-solving. Imagine a 'coding' task, where one is given a list of twenty-six unfamiliar and difficult-to-name symbols, one for each letter of the alphabet (a = ℘, b = Ӡ, c = ⊗, d = ∩, etc.) and asked to 'translate' a passage of text into the symbols. After an hour or so it seems probable that most people would

be familiar with all the symbols and remember how they correspond to the letters of the alphabet, and so be able to translate
quickly and fluently. They would have *automatised* their performance, and would be able to carry out the task without having
to concentrate hard on it.

It is possible to measure the degree to which an individual
has automatised a task by estimating how much attention-span
is left over for other activities. For example, whilst performing
the translation task (the 'primary task') the participants might
also be asked to solve mental arithmetic problems presented via
headphones. The test instructions would stress that quick and
accurate performance on the translation task is the most important aspect of the experiment, and that the arithmetic problems
(the 'secondary task') should just be attempted if this does not
interfere with performance on the primary task. Other (arguably
better) techniques have also been developed (e.g. Mulhern, 1997).

This sub-theory therefore tries to identify which aspects of
tests and test-items make them useful measures of intelligence.
Most tests will involve a mixture of highly automatised skills
and novel skills, and Sternberg (1985) suggests that tests and
test-items measuring the second-order factor of fluid ability
(Gf) typically measure individual differences in solving novel problems (e.g. analogies, identifying the next number in a series)
whilst those that tap crystallised ability (Gc) determine how well
automatised certain operations have become (e.g. reading comprehension).

An overview of Sternberg's work

Sternberg's theory is valuable in that it attempts to expand the
definition of 'intelligence' away from the somewhat arbitrary set
of mental tasks developed by psychometricians. Furthermore, as
any task will require the use of high-level planning strategies
(metacomponents), this might well explain why so many different
tasks all load on one factor (g). General ability may reflect
individual differences in the efficiency of people's metacomponents: a view which is somewhat at odds with theories considered

in Chapter 5 that suggest that g is related to speed/efficiency of neuronal information transmission.

The theory also attempts to explain what is going on when people solve problems – in either in the laboratory or real life. The componential sub-theory is an enormously important attempt to integrate the psychology of abilities with cognitive psychology and human learning processes. It tries to model which elementary cognitive operations (each of which take a person a certain, characteristic, amount of time) are performed in which sequence as a person solves a reasoning problem. It seeks to explain abilities in terms of cognitive processes. However, the amount of time taken to perform various elementary cognitive operations turns out to be difficult to assess, and the durations of ECOs estimated from one task fail to predict performance on other tasks. Metacomponents are thought to be important for understanding human learning, but as with some of the cognitive components, it is not obvious that all aspects of the theory can be falsified. Thus it is questionable whether the componential sub-theory is scientific.

The contextual sub-theory requires intelligent behaviour to be influenced by a huge range of social, cultural and personal factors (including personality, motivation, values and mood), and the experiential sub-theory has attempted to explain the solution of 'insight problems' (which require selective encoding/combination of information in a novel problem) and the precise role of experience in problem-solving. Furthermore, the these sub-theories try to understand what is 'intelligent' behaviour within real-life settings, rather than in trivial laboratory tasks. It also seeks to explain why there may be group and cultural differences in test performance (for example, abstract geometric shapes may be relatively unfamiliar to members of some cultures) or in automatising complex sequences of cognitive operations. However, Kline (1991) observes that several aspects of the theory are non-contingent concepts, and are hence untestable, whilst the unlimited complexity of the componential sub-theory means that it is difficult to test in practice. One reviewer is even more ascerbic:

things like 'recognition of just what the nature of the problem is' and 'understanding of internal and external feedback concerning the quality of task performance' are not separate elements in any genuine mental process; they are more like chapter headings in books on how to think.

(Neisser, 1983)

To understand the components and metacomponents requires experiments, not lists.

Howard Gardner's theory of multiple intelligences

The 'psychometric model' of abilities outlined in Chapter 2 is what cognitive psychologists would call a bottom-up or data-driven model. Factor analysis is used to determine how many abilities are necessary to explain people's performance on a wide but fairly arbitrary selection of mental tests. And so there are plenty of phenomena that this model was not designed to explain – for example, the abilities of 'unusual groups', such as geniuses, brain-damaged individuals or children with severe learning difficulties. Nor does it seek to explain how and why abilities develop over time, nor indeed the processes that *cause* individual differences in these abilities to emerge in the first place (for although some such models are examined above and in Chapters 4 and 5 these do not spring from the data-driven model of factor analysis).

Gardner, on the other hand, has set out some criteria that he regards as essential for a theory of ability *within a particular culture*. For like Sternberg, Gardner is careful to emphasise that what is regarded as 'intelligent' may vary drastically from culture to culture. So he views intelligence as being adequacy of performance at whatever is valued in a culture. Abilities such as catching fish, memorising a holy book and making money will be valued differently by different cultures: thus the definition of what makes 'intelligent' behaviour must also change from culture to culture.

Unusually, Gardner also regards 'intelligence' behaviourally: intelligence is what a person can *do*. So possessing (and knowing how to use) a computer, having access to a telephone and having friends from whom one can learn or 'bounce ideas' would make an individual more intelligent, according to this definition (Gardner, 1993: xvii). More traditional views of general ability try to minimise individual differences in the methods used to solve problems, for example by devising problems that are solved by individuals (not collaborating groups of people) where equipment (e.g. a computer) is either made available to everyone or to no one taking the test. The testing situation is made as standard as possible for each person being assessed, as it is thought that variables such as computer-use and telephone-use will be influenced by economic factors, thus making the test-items easier for those with access to such aids. More fundamentally, traditional ability tests assume that everyone tackling the items set about them in much the same way. Gardner's approach (in which 'intelligent' performance on a vocabulary test could result from a good vocabulary, access to a dictionary/electronic thesaurus or good advice from a friend) implies that different people can use quite different skills to solve the problems. How reasonable is it to compare the scores of people who solve problems in quite different ways? If someone walks three miles in an hour, does this mean that this person has less 'movement ability' than someone who cycles it in ten minutes, or drives it in five?

Gardner's work ignores one of the main findings of factor-analytic research – g. Instead he claims 'that there exists a multitude of intelligences, quite independent of each other' (1993: xxiii). Yet this is surely an *empirical* matter rather than an assumption: it is difficult to see why the theory would be infirmed if the various intelligences were found to be correlated. He believes that the only reason why there are correlations between the various primary and secondary abilities (such as discussed in Chapter 2) is because all these tests rely on the use of language or logic. A child who is good at language/logic will perform well at all of them; a child who has difficulties with language/logic will perform poorly at all of them. According to Gardner, if we were to control for ('partial out' is the statistical term) the effects of language and logic from ability tests, the intelligence factors would really be uncorrelated. This view is slightly surprising given that some primary and secondary abilities – e.g. memory for strings of digits, pairs of random letters, pitch perception, spatial ability, visualisation – do not seem to rely extensively on either language *or* logic. And if Gardner's explanation were correct, how could there possibly more than one or two second-order factors (corresponding to language ability and/or logical ability)?

Gardner rejects factor analysis as a tool for determining the structure of abilities on the basis of some rather specious arguments put forward in Steven Jay Gould's book, *The Mismeasure of Man* (Gould, 1981).[1] Instead, Gardner suggests that an 'intelligence' should be identified by:

(a) abilities that all disappear (or are all retained) following damage to some area(s) of the brain
(b) abilities that are found together is prodigies or those with severe learning difficulties ('idiots savant')
(c) a genetically programmed set of cognitive operations that operate on particular stimuli (e.g. those involved in pitch-perception, or imitation)
(d) clear development of the system as the child ages
(e) tasks that interfere with each other (in dual-task experiments) or which transfer together to new situations – and so which are likely to share a common neural mechanism
(f) intercorrelations between psychometric tests measuring these cognitive operations
(g) the development of systems of symbols to represent concepts – e.g. language, mathematics, music.

Thus, rather than focusing on a single type of evidence, Gardner draws on physiological psychology, several aspects of cognitive

---

[1] This is widely regarded as a seriously misleading and partial book that is frequently factually incorrect, and is 'crafted in such a way as to prejudice the general public and even some scientists against almost any research concerning human cognitive abilities' (Carroll, 1995): the rest of this review from one of the most widely respected figures in individual differences research contains even stronger phrases, and I would urge anyone who has read Gould's book to also consult this review.

psychology, developmental psychology and clinical psychology in order to find groups of abilities that seemed to come and go together. These, he believes, constitute different forms of 'intelligence'. Gardner then searched the psychological and medical literature to try to find 'intelligences' that conformed to these criteria. In total he identified seven classes of 'intelligence' that met most or all of them. These were linguistic intelligence, musical intelligence, logical-mathematical intelligence, spatial intelligence, bodily-kinaesthetic intelligence, and two forms of personal intelligence (integrity of self-concept and quality of interactions with others). They are described in some detail in *Frames of Mind* (Gardner, 1993) along with some fascinating suggestions about how certain historical figures (ranging from Freud to Gandhi) exemplarise particular abilities. I do not propose to discuss these 'intelligences' further here – not because they are uninteresting, but because the first four of them seem to correspond very closely to some of the main ability traits identified by factor analysts, and discussed in Chapter 2. The other three (bodily-kinaesthetic intelligence, which is concerned with co-ordination and grace of movements, and intrapersonal and interpersonal intelligence) probably would not be regarded as *mental* abilities under some definitions of the term. Thus, whilst Gardner's work is useful in that it adopts a completely different approach to the mapping of human abilities, it seems that this work reinforces what the factor-theorists had already suggested.

One problem with Gardner's approach is that it is not obvious that the list of 'intelligences' is complete. There may be others that have not been identified. Sexual performance is one variable that has a clear developmental trend, can be affected by damage to certain areas of the brain or by drugs (e.g. alcohol), is very highly regarded within some cultures, has its own set of symbols, and so on. So why is there no factor of sexual intelligence?

Gardner's theories have become extremely popular, particularly with teachers and educators, as they paint a much more positive, egalitarian picture than the hierarchical model outlined in Chapter 2. For if there *are* a number of completely separate 'intelligences', if a child has difficulty in one area (e.g. linguistic or logical-mathematical intelligence) then the teacher could and should look around for areas of strength that can be developed. If the various intelligences are uncorrelated, very few children will be seriously below average in all of them. However, the positive correlations between the ability factors that are implied by the hierarchical model suggests that if children are below average in one area, they are unlikely to excel in others. There will be some variation in performance, but it is most unlikely that a child who is one or two standard deviations below the mean on verbal or mathematical ability will be one or two standard deviations above the mean on anything else.

Like Guilford's (1967) theory of the 'structure of intellect', which also postulated a theoretical model of ability (rather than examining the actual correlations between tests and between factors), there is really rather little empirical evidence to support Gardner's crucial claim that the various 'intelligences' are independent. Without this, his theory seems to be entirely compatible with the hierarchical models considered in Chapter 2.

Intelligence as explanation?

Michael Howe (1988b) published an article with the title 'Intelligence as explanation'. It and his latest book (Howe, 1997) raise some important questions about the nature of abilities, two of which we shall deal with here, and others in subsequent chapters.

The circularity of the concept of 'intelligence'

Can it ever be legitimate to claim (as some authors do) that people behave in a certain way *because* they have certain levels of certain abilities? According to Howe (1997, 1988b) this is not possible. Psychologists such as Spearman, Thurstone and Cattell make the mistake of:

(a) using factor analysis to note some consistencies in behaviour (e.g. that a child performs well at a great number of cognitive tasks)

(b) concluding that one or more ability factors (such as g) describe this performance

(c) suggesting that the *reason* why the child performs well on these tasks is because they have high levels of g.

The problem arises at step (c). Suppose that we measured and weighed a random sample of books from a typical bookshelf. It would probably be found that the height, weight and thickness of the books formed a factor, which we could call 'size'. Can we now say that the reason why some books differ from others in their height/weight/thickness is that they have different values of 'size'? Obviously not! Size is a *property* of the books, not a *reason* for their different measurements. (The reason why books differ in size is closely related to the number of words and/or pictures in them.) Following this analogy through, it is completely wrong to try to explain behaviour by suggesting that people have different scores on various factors. This is sometimes known as a **circular explanation**.

Yet the picture may not be as bleak as painted above. Suppose that one measures some behaviours in a college bar late on Saturday night. The behaviours that are assessed include volubility of talking, ability to perform finely co-ordinated actions, and a self-assessment of well-being. It seems very likely that the more that individuals have been drinking, the more they will tend to talk, show poor co-ordination and report that they feel wonderful. Thus, if these behaviours are assessed in people who have been drinking to different extents, the behaviours will be found to form a factor. The presence of a factor indicates that these three aspects of behaviour share a common cause – alcohol.

It may well be the same with abilities. The finding that a group of abilities tend to rise and fall together (and hence form a factor) when different people are compared suggests that they have a common origin – though whether this is biological, cognitive, social or educational remains to be determined. In other words, the very presence of a factor may be evidence that some more fundamental process is at work.[2] If so, it may be quite reasonable to use the factor as an explanation. To say that people slur and stagger 'because they are drunk' is quite legitimate once we know that 'drunkenness' has its roots in a simple chemical. This is why it is vitally important to discover the processes underlying ability factors.

Why do some people perform better than others on tests measuring inductive reasoning, spatial ability, *g*, etc.? Is it possible that there is something 'inside the individual' that *causes* them to behave at a certain, characteristic level on a particular set of tasks? Sternberg's work suggests that there are unlikely to be any gross differences in the durations of ECOs between people, but could there be other explanations? Quality of schooling is an obvious contender for tasks measuring crystallised ability, or any of its components (numerical and verbal abilities, mechanical knowledge) as a child who has never been taught to read, write or gain knowledge about the operation of cogs, pulleys or tools, for example, will be unable to perform well on such tasks. In the case of many other abilities, there is now excellent evidence that our genes play an important part in determining our ultimate level of performance. As genes can produce only various types of proteins, this necessarily implies that some biological processes are at work, as also suggested by much of Gardner's work, mentioned above. Theories of the genetic and biological basis of abilities are developed in Chapter 4 and 5.

To summarise, Howe argues that whilst ability factors may provide useful descriptions of behaviour, they are nothing more than this. They do not imply any corresponding functional or structural mechanisms (Howe calls them 'faculties') inside an individual's head. Sternberg (1988) counters that as several abilities show modest to substantial correlations with other biological and cognitive measures, scores on ability tests probably reflect genuine

---

[2] It 'may be' evidence rather than 'is' evidence, for this logic breaks down where the variables being factor analysed are highly similar in content – e.g. five tests measuring performance at number-series, rather than tapping a wide range of reasoning tasks.

individual differences in brain structure and function. Viewed like this, ability tests are rather like diagnostic indicators in the physical and biochemical sciences. The finding that an acid turns litmus paper red is, in itself, one of the least interesting properties of acids. However, knowing that a liquid is an acid (as a result of the litmus test) allows one to predict what is likely to happen in other, much more important, chemical reactions. It is the same with ability factors and ability tests. If (and only if) a certain level of performance on a test measuring a particular ability factor can be reliably related to the individual's social/cognitive/educational/cultural/biological makeup, scores on the test may influence a much wider range of behaviours than those assessed by the particular test.

Such a model is shown in Figure 3.1. The single-headed arrows imply that some property of the individual influences both performance on the ability test and other, much more important, real-life performances. So if performance on ability tests reflects certain basic physiological/cognitive/ social/cultural or other processes then it is entirely sensible to explain behaviour in terns of abilities. Just like the litmus paper, the abilities that are

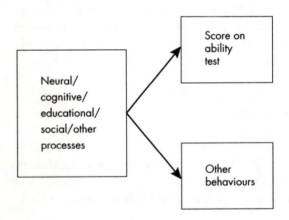

FIGURE 3.1 A model suggesting that scores on ability tests are determined by some structure or process inside the individual which also determines other behaviours

measured by a psychological test may indicate some more fundamental property of the individual (analogous to the H_3O^+ ion)
that will influence a wide range of behaviours (chemical reactions), and not just those that happen to be measured by the
diagnostic test.

Does g exist?

There is a problem with Howe's claim that 'there are no
convincing reasons at all for insisting that g [or presumably any
other ability factor] is something real' (Howe, 1988b: 30). This
presumably means that it does not reflect any cognitive/physio-
logical processes inside the individual. So what *does* determine a
child's performance on the various ability factors? Having ruled
out 'real' biological mechanisms, a child's cultural, social and
educational experiences seem to be all that are left. They may
reflect knowledge of facts, or basic taught skills (such as reading
and arithmetic). If this is so, then:

● one would presumably expect children from the same families, or those from the similar social background who attend
   the same schools, to show very little variation in ability.
   Some evidence in Chapter 4 shows that the first of these
   explanations is not well supported by the data.
● this model does not provide a plausible account of the structure of abilities. Consider Gs (spatial ability). Its items are
   abstract geometric forms. Children are likely to be exposed
   to such shapes during mathematics lessons at school. So
   if the amount of exposure/quality of education is all-
   important, why does the numerical ability primary not load
   the Gs factor? And how can the Gr (retrieval/creativity)
   factor emerge, since items in its constituent primary abilities (e.g. 'what useful object could you make from a candle,
   an apple and a pin?') bear little resemblance to anything
   taught at school or at home?

Howe's position

Howe has argued that whilst it is legitimate to use ability factors to describe how people behave, it is quite wrong to use them to *explain* behaviour: we should never say that 'John performs badly at school because he has low verbal ability', for example. Howe also suggests that as ability factors such as *g* are essentially social constructs, they do not 'exist' in any real form anywhere inside the individual. Authors such as Sternberg (1988) have suggested that the evidence is not so clear-cut as suggested by Howe, and I have shown that if scores on ability tests are merely taken as indicators of some more fundamental (perhaps biological) processes, then it seems quite possible that these processes may influence several different aspects of behaviour. And if they do *not* reflect basic biological processes, a purely social account is unlikely to produce the sort of structuring of abilities that was described in Chapter 2.

Summary

This chapter has examined three rather different alternatives to the factor-analytical models described in Chapter 2. Sternberg's theory suggests that abilities should be seen within a certain experiential and cultural context, although to do so is far from easy in practice, as this requires a detailed understanding of each individual's motivation, personality, values, etc. Sternberg's componential sub-theory might be useful, in that the higher-order planning components (metacomponents) may perhaps explain *g*. A person's ability to select appropriate strategies for problem-solving might explain why some individuals are more able than others at solving all kinds of cognitive problems, which is what *g* implies. Against that, some aspects of Sternberg's theory are non-testable in principle.

Gardner's theory provides a surprising amount of support for the psychometric model of ability outlined previously, despite considering rather different criteria. Four of his seven 'intelligences' seem similar to factors in the psychometric model, whilst the others (bodily-kinaesthetic and two forms of personal intelligence) have not traditionally been regarded as mental abilities by those who construct ability tests. Perhaps such measures should be included in future revisions of ability test batteries. Gardner's claim that his various 'intelligences' are *independent* of each other runs counter to the psychometric model, but this is, after all, an empirical rather than a theoretical issue.

Howe claims that factor analysis is unable to help identify the causes of behaviour: an idea about which I have some reservations. For as shown above, factor analysis may sometimes be able to reveal the presence of genuine causes of behaviour. It is thus vital to determine whether performance on tests measuring the main ability factors are substantially related to other, basic, cognitive, biological or other processes. If they are, then it may be legitimate to explain behaviour in terms of ability factors. Hence the two chapters that follow consider whether abilities have a genetic basis (i.e. whether a biological explanation of ability should be sought) and whether they are related to simple properties of nerves or cognitive processes.

Further reading

Gardner, H. (1993) *Frames of Mind* (2nd edn), London: HarperCollins. The theory of multiple intelligences.

Howe, M.J.A. (1988b) 'Intelligence as explanation', *British Journal of Psychology* 79: 349–360. An article arguing that general ability leads to circular explanations.

Sternberg, R.J. (1985) *Beyond IQ*, Cambridge: Cambridge University Press. An account of the triarchic theory.

Sternberg, R.J. (1988) 'Explaining away intelligence: a reply to Howe', *British Journal of Psychology* 79: 527–534. Sternberg's reply to Howe

The genetics of ability

THE GENETIC BASIS OF HUMAN abilities is one of the best-researched issues in the whole of psychology. Early individual-difference psychologists (e.g. Spearman, Burt, Terman) were well aware of the success of animal breeding programmes for developing certain psychological characteristics (e.g. aggressive versus docile behaviour in dogs) through selective breeding, and so were keen to consider the role that genetics played in determining a child's ultimate levels of intelligence. Many of these pioneers took a right-wing stance, suggesting that society would be improved if highly intelligent people were encouraged to have plenty of children, whilst less intelligent people should be actively discouraged (or prevented) from doing so. For as they believed that general ability was largely inherited, this course of action should increase the overall intelligence of the nation. This became known as the Eugenics movement; the Eugenics Society still exists today.

Despite this politically suspect past, the issue of the **heritability** of abilities is a perfectly legitimate scientific question. Tryon's (1940) work showed that it is possible to breed selectively two strains of rat ('maze-bright' and 'maze-dull'), one of which will quickly learn to run through mazes for food, whilst the other will not perform well in mazes. This was the first scientific study proving that a behaviour (maze-running) may be influenced by selective breeding. Thus, it seems reasonable to ask whether individual differences in any other types of ability (together with personality traits, attitudes, etc.) might perhaps be influenced by genetic makeup as well as environments in humans. In other words, might some individuals be predisposed to behave in certain ways, given suitable environmental conditions? This branch of psychology is known as **behaviour genetics**.

There is another method that is sometimes used to discover which **genes** influence various traits. Suppose that DNA is collected from a group of prodigies – those with exceptional musical talent, for example. It can be presumed that these individuals will have developed their skills only if they have both a genetic predisposition and a supportive environment. So if the DNA from members of this group is compared with the DNA of a control group of average musical ability, any consistent differences may point directly to individual genes that predispose an individual to musical greatness. Unlike the methods described below, this approach can identify precisely which genes on which chromosomes predispose children to particular behaviours. This approach has two main difficulties: the number of variable genes is so vast that it is very difficult to know which ones to compare between the two groups, and if many genes influence a particular trait, the effect of each (examined individually) will be rather small, particularly if genes also interact. Against this, it does provide a very precise picture of how genes operate, which is why workers such as Robert Plomin (e.g. Plomin *et al.*, 1995; Plomin and Petrill, 1997) actively pursue this line of research.

The basic aim of behaviour genetics is not to understand precisely which genes influence what, but to determine the extent to which certain behaviours (or, more commonly, traits) are influenced by our genetic makeup, and by various aspects of our environment. This leap from genetics to behaviour misses out many vitally important stages. After all, the only thing that *any* gene can do is produce a protein of one kind or another, and so if abilities are found to have a substantial genetic component this would suggest that individual differences in abilities may be related (somehow) to individual differences in the development or makeup of the nervous system. On the other hand, if individual differences in abilities are purely determined by our environments, it seems unlikely that studying individual differences in the biology of the nervous system will be of much help when researching the origins of these individual differences. It would be much more appropriate to study social and cognitive influences. Thus, one important outcome of the nature–nurture debate (as this is sometimes known) is to suggest promising routes for researching the correlates of abilities.

Basic theory

Humans are genetically highly similar: we all share well over 90 per cent of our genes with all other members of our species. However, the techniques of behaviour genetics described below focus on those genes that *do* show variability from person to person. Chromosomes are long (5 cm) strands of a protein called DNA that are tightly packed into the cell nucleus. Each of these strands of DNA comprises a long sequence of genes: chemicals that (in various ways) control the synthesis of amino acids and proteins. Twenty-three pairs of chromosomes are found in the nucleus of almost every cell in our bodies. When an egg is fertilised, the offspring receives half its chromosomes (and so half its genetic makeup) from the mother, and half from the father. If we assume that the parents are unrelated to each other (that is, share a chance number of the genes that vary from person to person) it follows that siblings share half the genetic material that varies in people. So does a parent and child. **Fraternal** ('dizygotic' or non-identical) **twins** result when two sperm fertilise two eggs: they too share half the genes that vary. It sometimes happens that the fertilised egg splits in two or more clumps of cells during the early stages of growth. These clumps of cells may each develop into an individual, and these people are genetically identical (we ignore any mutations in the womb) hence known as **identical twins.**

Genes can influence behaviour in several different ways. In the simplest case, each of a number of genes can have a small influence on some characteristic of the organism. For example, it might be that several genes determine height: the more of these genes that are present in an individual, the taller that person is likely to be (given a suitable environment: adequate nutrition, etc.). In other words the influence of the genes is additive. The more of these genes one has, the taller one is likely to be, and so this is known as the 'additive model'. Or genes can interact. It may be that a certain characteristic will emerge only if a person has *one or more* genes present at the same position in a pair of chromosomes. If the person has neither of them, then the characteristic will not be seen. Sometimes characteristics emerge only if certain genes are present at a *number* of different positions on the chromosome. Although the majority of the research to be discussed below assumes a simple additive model, behaviour geneticists are actively researching more complex models too.

The environment, too, may well influence behaviour. Two types of environmental influences have traditionally been studied. The first, the **common environment** (also known as the shared environment), describes all those features of the environment that are shared by all the brothers and sisters in a family. For example, parental income, parental attitudes to education, the parents' behaviour and style of child-rearing, the number of books in the house and the type of food provided is likely to be broadly similar for all the children in one family, assuming that levels of income are stable and that the parents stay together. Sharing a common environment will tend to make members of the same family behave in similar ways. Each child also has a **unique environment**; individual children will develop their own friends, may each be influenced by a different teacher at school, may develop different hobbies and skills, and miss different chunks of schooling because of childhood illnesses. The unique environment describes those environmental influences that will tend to make members of a family *different* from each other.

The basic aim of all the studies considered below is to determine the extent to which individual differences in behaviour (or some trait, such as general ability) are influenced by individual differences in genetic makeup, and individual differences in the common environment and the unique environment. For example, we may wish to discover the relative importance of the common environment, the unique environment and genetic makeup on children's levels of spatial ability. However, before going on to discuss some research designs, it is important to appreciate what this approach implies.

(a) Estimates of the relative importance of genes, the common environment and the unique environment will depend on who is tested. If these are unrepresentative of the population (e.g. by excluding homeless, substance-abusing and institutionalised individuals) then it will be unwise to extrapolate estimates of the relative importance of the common and unique environments and genetic influences to the general population.

(b)   Heritability estimates are based on the range of environments that are usually found in a society, and so should not be applied cross-culturally. For example, if the range of environments experienced by children in some cultures varies far more than in our society (some children going hungry, suffering disease and living in squalor whilst others are enjoying an affluent lifestyle) this will affect the relative importance of environmental and genetic influences.

(c)   Even if an ability is 100 per cent genetically determined, it can still be changed by environmental intervention: it may well be possible to boost (or lower) children's levels of general ability, through environmental manipulations. But can the *rank-ordering* of children be easily manipulated? The examples used by those who focus on these issues (e.g. Howe, 1997: 114) assume that low-performing children move up the ranking because they receive an effective intervention, whereas those ranked just above them do not receive any sort of intervention. Were *all* children to receive the intervention, we might well expect all of them to improve: it is difficult to imagine that if a truly effective intervention were discovered it would be made available only to those with the very lowest levels of ability.

(d)   The relative importance of the common and unique environments and genetic makeup are features of the *sample*, not of the *individual*: it would be meaningless to claim that about half of a particular child's intelligence is determined by the environment and about half by the parents' genetic makeup, for example.

(e)   Whilst early studies ignored the age of participants, it is now thought vital to conduct developmental studies to investigate the development of abilities over the lifespan, as the importance of the family is likely to be greater at some ages than others, whilst certain genes may influence behaviour only at certain ages. And what of experience? Even if some individuals start life with some genetically endowed advantage, are these benefits outweighed by environmental factors (such as quality of education, work experience) by the time one reaches adulthood? Or do early genetic advantages continue through life?

Behaviour-genetic studies of abilities

The literature here is vast, and has been summarised in a great many thoughtful reviews and empirical reports (e.g. Bouchard, 1995; Bouchard and McGue, 1981; Neisser *et al.*, 1996; Pedersen and Lichtenstein, 1997; Plomin and McClearn, 1993; Scarr and Carter-Saltzman, 1982; Thompson, 1993). In this section I have stressed the types of methodologies used, and given one or two examples of some typical results. Other results will be found in the sources listed above. Most of the studies have focused on measures of general ability, g, rather than primary or secondary abilities. The reasons for focusing on g rather than primary or secondary abilities are generally obscure.

If general ability has a substantial genetic basis, then individuals who are genetically similar should (other things being equal) show similar levels of general ability. Thus, identical twins (who share *all* their genes) should have very similar scores on tests of general ability. Fraternal twins, brothers and sisters, or a parent and a child (each of whom share half their variable genetic material) should be rather less similar. Uncles/aunts and their nephews/nieces (who share a quarter of their variable genes) should be less similar and so on. Thus, one approach might be to test whether closely related individuals tend to have levels of general ability that are more similar than less closely related individuals. The problem is that gathering these kinds of data is difficult, as it is necessary to study relatives who never see each other – otherwise the correlations might arise because of common environment, rather than shared genes alone.

Adoption studies are much easier to work with. If the family environment is an important factor in developing a child's general ability, then one might expect all children – even unrelated children – who are reared in the same family environment to develop similar levels of general ability. Children who are removed from their families shortly after birth and adopted into another family may thus give valuable information about the importance of the common environment for intelligence. Adopted children will share few genes (other than those that all humans have in common) with other children in the family. They will also (by definition) not share their unique environment with other family members. So if it is found that adopted children tend to have levels of some ability that are similar to other members of the family, then this provides good evidence that the common environment is important for the development of this ability. Several large-scale studies (Bouchard, 1993 gives references) have been instigated to keep track of adoptees, such as the Texas Adoption Study, the Colorado Adoption Study, the Minnesota Adoption Study, and the Swedish Adoption/Twin Study of Ageing.

In order to test the importance of the common environment it is necessary to trace several hundred adopted children, measure their level of ability, measure the level of ability of *other* children in the same families, and use a statistic called the 'semipartial correlation' to decide whether the variation *within* families is smaller than the variation *between* families, as one would expect if the family environment is all-important for determining levels of the ability.

The evidence shows that in childhood, adopted children do tend to have similar levels of general ability to other members of the adoptive family. However, they become less (rather than more) similar to other children in the family as they grow up. Loehlin *et al.* (1989) analysed data from the Texas Adoption Study comparing the general ability of adopted children and other children within the same family – both fellow-adoptees and biological offspring of the adoptive parents. The childhood correlations of 0.11 and 0.20 (which indicate the influence of the common environment) fell to –0.09 and 0.05 ten years later, when the children were aged between 13 and 24. This suggests that the influence of the family environment becomes negligible as the children grow into adulthood. Where the adoptive parents have two children of their own, the correlation between *their* levels of general ability (which are influenced by both the family environment *and* their genetic similarity) is 0.27 in childhood and 0.24 ten years later. This suggests that genes may influence ability.

Thus, it seems that children have similar levels of general ability in adulthood only if they are biologically related. Merely being brought up in the same family seems to have little influence on adult levels of *g*. This study suggests that both the common environment and genetic makeup affects general ability in childhood, but the influence of the common environment declines in adulthood whilst genetic influences endure. Plomin and Daniels (1987) report much the same thing, from a different sample of twins. The data are also entirely consistent with the earlier work of Skodak and Skeels (1949). Extrapolating to the general population, this suggests that the common environment ('family ethos') simply fails to influence levels of general ability in adulthood.

This is not to say that the environment does not matter. Heritability figures refer to children *in general* in the sorts of environments that are *typically* found in Western society. Severely deprived or abusive environments may, and probably *do*, have a severe influence on individual children's intellectual development. But if such environments are relatively rare in our culture, this will not show up once the scores of all the well-treated children are averaged in with those of the deprived minority. But in general, the home environment has a surprisingly modest influence on children's ultimate levels of general ability.

What of the link between the adopted children's levels of general ability, and the levels of general ability of their biological and adoptive parents? Children's levels of general ability are related to that of both their adoptive mothers (r = 0.13) and their biological mothers (r = 0.23, N ≥ 200: Loehlin *et al.*, 1989). Ten years later, adults/adolescents who had been adopted still showed a similar degree of correlation between their level of general ability and that of their biological mother. However, the correlation with their adopted mothers' general ability fell to 0.05, whilst that with their biological mothers' ability remained unchanged (r = 0.26). This too suggests that the influence of the common environment on general ability is negligible by adulthood.

Segal (1997) traced twenty-one pairs of non-related individuals of the same age (mean difference = 83 days) who were brought up together since shortly after birth (mean delay = 39 days). She argued that the way in which these pairs were brought up strongly resembles the way that non-identical twins are brought up (non-identical rather than identical, as the unrelated individuals do not look alike). Thus, they share many aspects of their early environments. Most of the sample were tested at age 4–6, but some were aged over 20 at the time of testing. The correlation between the general ability of these pairs is a direct estimate of the contribution of the shared environment to general ability – albeit over a rather large range of ages – as these children share no variable genes. Other controls were good; for example, two different psychologists administered the tests to each pair of individuals, so ensuring that any similarity was not due to some form of 'tester bias'. The correlation between these pairs of unrelated individuals was found to be 0.17 – substantially below the figures usually reported for pairs of fraternal twins brought up together, for whom Bouchard and McGue's (1981) meta-analysis suggested a correlation of 0.60, based on 5,546 pairs of twins. So from this study too it appears that individuals are substantially more similar in terms of their general ability if they share more genes.

Quantitative genetics

The interpretations given in the previous section were qualitative in nature. The influence of the shared environment was estimated by calculating correlations between adopted children and others, and some estimate of the relative importance of genetic factors and the shared environment might perhaps be drawn by comparing the size of the correlations between the children and their biological mothers, or members of their adoptive family. However, we have not yet tried to quantify these influences.

The aim of quantitative genetic studies is to determine (for a given population, experiencing a particular variety of environments) the relative importance of shared genes, the shared environment, and the unique environment for determining children's behaviour, or their level of some trait. In the following sections I shall derive some very simple formulae for estimating the relative importance of genetic and environmental influences on any behaviour or trait. I do so to demonstrate how simple correlations between pairs of twins and other family members can be used to draw powerful inferences about the relative importance of genetic and environmental influences on ability. Should you be expected to reproduce these equations it will be easier to derive them as needed, rather than relying on memory.

Adoption studies

Denoting the genetic contribution as A, the common (shared) environment as C and the unique environment as E, we first assume that

$$\text{Total variation} = A + C + E = 1 \qquad \text{Equation 4.1}$$

That is, that the common environment, the unique environment and genes together explain all the variation in an ability. The figures A, C and E thus represent the relative importance of these three influences.

Adoptive children share half their variable genes with their biological mother (or father), and none with their adoptive mother (or, equivalently, the adoptive father, or the offspring of the adoptive parents). Consider a child brought up by the biological mother. Since they share half their variable genes, and the common environment and the child's unique environment will also influence its level of general ability, we may write

$$r_{bc} = \frac{A}{2} + C \qquad\qquad \text{Equation 4.2}$$

where r_{bc} denotes the correlation between the general ability of the biological mother and the child. Note that E does not appear in this equation – or in any of those that follow – as the mother does not (by definition) share the unique environment with her child.

For an adopted child, we can write (for reasons that should be obvious)

$$r_{mc} = 0 + C \qquad\qquad \text{Equation 4.3}$$

as the adopted child shares a common environment (but no variable genes) with other members of the family.

Subtracting Equation 4.3 from Equation 4.2 gives

$$r_{bc} - r_{mc} = \frac{A}{2} \text{ and thus}$$

$$A = 2(r_{bc} - r_{mc}) \qquad\qquad \text{Equation 4.4}$$

Thus, if we know the correlation between the test scores of adoptive children and one of their parents, and the correlation between the test scores of normally raised children and one of *their* parents, these figures can be inserted into Equation 4.4 to estimate the proportion of variance in general ability that is genetically transmitted.

We have not mentioned a figure for r_{mc} earlier in the chapter: however, Bouchard and McGue (1981) report a result (averaged across a number of studies) of 0.42. So how heritable is general ability? Assuming r_{mc} to be 0.42, and r_{ma} in the children to be 0.13 (as mentioned in the text above), we estimate the heritability of general ability for children to be $(0.42 - 0.13) \times 2$, or 0.58. That is, inherited genes explain rather more than half of the variation in general ability within this population.

It is also possible to estimate the relative importance of the shared and the non-shared environments – indeed, Equation 4.3

shows this directly. So here the common environment explains 13 per cent of the variation of general ability. Note how close this is to the 0.17 that was inferred from Segal's (1997) adoption study (discussed above). The remaining $100 - 58 - 13 = 29$ per cent of the variation is due to individual differences in the children's unique environments (see Equation 4.1).

The models applied here (which stem from the work of Jinks and Fulker, 1970) are very simple, and fail to take into account any non-additive genetic effects, which will lead the above equations to overestimate the importance of genetic influences. Nor can they allow for the possibility that foster children may not be treated *exactly* the same as other members of the family. More complex models have been derived to take account of these difficulties; P. E. Vernon (1979) describes some of the older models, and Stevenson (1997) and Pedersen and Lichtenstein (1997) discuss some new approaches, based on a statistical method known as path analysis.

Twins reared together and apart

Much research in genetics has focused on twins, as pairs of identical twins reared in the same family share the same genetic makeup and shared environment, whilst non-identical (fraternal) twins reared together form a useful control groups: they too shared the same environment from conception onward, as well as having all the environmental similarities caused by being the same age. Most studies consider only fraternal twins who are the same gender, to provide a still better match. Major twin studies include those based on the Swedish Adoption/Twin Study of Aging (e.g. Plomin and McClearn, 1990), the Louisville Longitudinal Twin Study (Wilson, 1983), the Western Reserve Twin Project (Thompson, 1993), the MacArthur Longitudinal Twin Study (Plomin *et al.*, 1990) and the Twin Infant Project (DiLalla *et al.*, 1990). There are also many older studies, summarised by Bouchard and McGue (1981).

We must at this point mention the 'Burt affair'. In the 1970s it was found that Sir Cyril Burt's twin data (important, as it contained so many pairs of separated twins) were not to be trusted. Not to put too fine a point on it, some of the numbers appeared to have been altered; Hearnshaw (1979) describes the scandal in some detail. Thus, it is important to ensure that Burt's data are ignored when drawing inferences about the general ability of twins – even though Burt's (probably fraudulent) data rather closely resemble the findings from later, reliable, studies.

Identical twins reared together share all their genes and their common environment. Using the convention where r_{mz} indicates the correlation between pairs of monozygotic (identical) twins and r_{dz} the correlation between dizygotic (fraternal) twins, we may write:

$$r_{mz} = A + C \qquad \text{Equation 4.5}$$

whilst non-identical twins share just half their genes and their common environment, so

$$r_{dz} = \frac{A}{2} + C \qquad \text{Equation 4.6}$$

Subtracting Equation 4.6 from Equation 4.5 gives

$$r_{mz} - r_{dz} = \frac{A}{2} + C - A - C = \frac{A}{2}$$

and multiplying both sides by 2 gives

$$2\,(r_{mz} - r_{dz}) = A \qquad \text{Equation 4.7}$$

So to estimate the heritability of a trait from twins reared together, one simply subtracts the correlation between the test scores of pairs of non-identical twins from the correlation between the test scores of pairs of identical twins, and doubles the result. To estimate the importance of the shared environment, C, both sides of Equation 4.6 may be doubled and then Equation 4.5 subtracted from it, giving

$$2r_{dz} - r_{mz} = A + 2C - A - C = C \qquad \text{Equation 4.8}$$

whilst the importance of the unique environment can be estimated (using Equation 4.1, Equation 4.5 and Equation 4.7) as

$$E = 1 - C - A$$

$$= 1 - (2r_{dz} - r_{mz}) - 2(r_{mz} - r_{dz})$$

$$= 1 - 2r_{dz} + r_{mz} - 2r_{mz} + 2r_{dz}$$

$$= 1 - r_{mz} \qquad \text{Equation 4.9}$$

Thus, it is possible to estimate the relative importance of the genes, common environment and unique environment for determining the general ability of a member of a certain society simply through inserting the correlations between pairs of identical (monozygotic) and fraternal (dizygotic) twins who have been reared together into Equations 4.7, 4.8 and 4.9.

What does the literature show? Bouchard and McGue (1981) famously summarised 111 older family studies of general ability and worked out average correlations for identical and non-identical twins reared together and apart, amongst others. Thompson (1993) reviews some of the more recent work. Bouchard and McGue (1981) reported that levels of general ability of pairs of non-identical twins reared in the same family correlated 0.60 (based on 5,546 pairs), whilst for identical twins brought up together the correlation was 0.86 (4,672 pairs). This implies (as you should verify, using Equations 4.7–4.9) that general ability has a heritability of approximately 52 per cent, with the shared environment and the unique environment accounting for 34 per cent and 14 per cent of the variation respectively. However, these studies averaged across several age ranges, which is undesirable given what is now known about how heritability changes with age. Thompson (1993: 112) estimates heritability to be 50 per cent in 6–12 year olds, with the shared and unique environments accounting for 42 per cent and 8 per cent of the variation – figures that agree well with the earlier studies.

Studies involving separated twins are even easier to understand. Two identical twins who are separated shortly after birth and reared in different environments will share only their genes. So for separated twins, $A = r_{mz}$. For separated dizygotic twins, $A = 2r_{dz}$. Bouchard *et al.* (1990) report values of r_{mz} ranging from 0.69 to 0.78 between pairs of identical twins who were reared apart and then given three tests of general ability. This implies that genes account for up to three-quarters of the variation in general ability. However, very few identical twins *are* separated at birth, and so the numbers are small (fewer than fifty in the above study). Furthermore, those twins who do manage (or choose) to find their identical twin and volunteer for testing may not be a representative sample of the population. Thus I would caution against making too much of the separated identical twin data – although curiously this is the only sort of behaviour-genetic study discussed and criticised by Howe (1997).

Several studies have tested twins repeatedly over their lifespan in order to determine whether general ability becomes 'swamped' by the effects of life experiences as one gets older, or whether an early genetic advantage endures. The usual finding is that the heritability of general ability increases steadily, peaking at a value of about 0.7–0.8 at age 40 (Pedersen and Lichtenstein, 1997), and then declining, perhaps because of variability in the onset of senile decay. Somewhat confusingly, the heritability of *g* seems to vary as a function of year of birth (as well as age): groups of Norwegian twins who were born in different years were tested at the same chronological age by Sundet *et al.* (1988) and the heritabilities were found to cycle up and down. No one really understands why this should be the case.

Methodological objections

Not everyone agrees with the interpretation of the data given above. Kamin (1974), Rose *et al.* (1984), Richardson (1991) and Howe

(1997) are amongst those who raise a number of criticisms of this work. They highlight important concerns about some aspects of the studies which may weaken their findings. For example

(a) At what age were children adopted into other families? If late in childhood, it may be the influence of the shared environment during some crucial early period (rather than shared genes) that makes the adoptees similar in later life.

(b) Adoptive families tend to be vetted by social service agencies, and so few children are likely to be adopted into extremely poor or abusive homes. The range of adoptive environments will be reduced, and this will lead to the importance of the common environment being underestimated.

(c) Selective placement may be a problem: children from working-class mothers may be adopted into working-class homes, whilst those from middle-class mothers may end up in middle-class homes. Hence the correlations between the biological mothers' and the adopted children's level of general ability may reflect similarities of social class (shared environment) and not genetic similarity.

(d) Do 'separated' twins truly never see each other, or might they live close to each other, meet at family gatherings (if adopted by a family member) and even attend the same schools? If so, it could be this contact (rather than genes) that makes them similar.

(e) Might identical twins who are raised together have similar levels of ability because they are often mistaken for each other, and basically treated much more similarly by teachers and parents than are non-identical twins?

(f) Perhaps children put up for adoption do not form a representative sample of the population. They may well have been abused, and the very process of adoption may be traumatic for the child.

(g) The psychologists administering the tests may 'encourage' twin-pairs to perform well, so manufacturing support for a genetic explanation.

Bouchard (1993) and Brody and Crowley (1995) discuss some of the points made briefly below, and provide data to demonstrate their validity.

(a) Some children in the older studies *were* adopted quite late in life, so the similarity to the biological mother might be explained by their sharing an environment for several years, rather than sharing genes. However, several modern studies are based on babies adopted during the first year of life; babies adopted earlier than six months show the same results as babies adopted a little later (Bouchard, 1993) and, in any case, adoption studies and family studies yield similar findings. Also, if crucial early-lifetime experiences (rather than genes) explain why children who are adopted into different families show similar levels of ability, why should adopted children become less similar to their adoptive families over time? And why is the relationship with the biological parent so strong?

(b) If restriction of range of the shared (adoptive) environment was a real problem, then there could not be an appreciable correlation between the scores of adoptees and other family members during childhood.

(c) Selective placement cannot be the full explanation, for why should the correlation between the biological parents' and adoptees' general ability remain constant over time, whilst the correlations between the adopted children and their adoptive parents and other members of the adoptive family decrease? If only one mechanism (shared environment) is at work, all three sets of correlations should change in similar ways. In any case, more recent studies (e.g. Bouchard *et al.*, 1990) now statistically control for the effects of selective placement, which is assessed by correlating the adoptive and biological parents' IQ and social class indices, physical facilities, educational achievement, etc. It has been found that although the parents' and the adoptive environments generally are correlated, neither of these is a good predictor of the children's level of general ability (Bouchard *et al.*, 1990).

(d)   Some supposedly 'separated' twins *were* in contact with each other in the early studies. However, later work (e.g. Bouchard *et al.*, 1990) took care to ensure that twins really were reared independently, and came to exactly the same conclusions as the earlier studies.

(e)   Monozygotic twins are unlikely to become alike because they are treated more similarly by their families than are dizygotic twins. Baker & Daniels (1990) found no relationship between the ways in which monozygotic twins were treated when young and their later similarity, and little variation in the ways in which parents treated monozygotic and dizygotic twins.

(f)   It is quite possible that adoptive children do *not* form a representative sample of the population, are more likely to have been abused, and may suffer distress at the adoption process. But why should this cause them to have similar levels of general ability to their biological mother? Or virtually no similarity to other same-aged children adopted into the family at the same time?

(g)   Twins are now tested by different investigators who are unaware of the other twin's score. Anyway, encouraging twin-pairs to perform well will not necessarily improve the correlation: to do so it would be better to encourage some twin-pairs to perform well, and others to perform badly!

All of the above objections suggest that the importance of genetic factors may have been overestimated. Yet there are also some important problems with the design of some of the experiments that may lead them to *underestimate* the role of genes. For example:

(a)   Test scores all have some measurement error associated with them. The effect of this will be to underestimate the true correlations between individuals. It can be shown (applying the formula on p. 220 of Nunnally, 1978 to Equation 4.7) that this will lead to the underestimation of genetic effects.

(b)   We do not select partners at random, but may choose others who share our interests – and level of general mental ability.

It has been found that pairs of partners have a correlation of 0.33 to 0.45 between their levels of *g* (Brody, 1992: 130). If there *is* a genetic component to general ability, this is likely to mean that the parents are likely to share some of the 'variable' genes that influence general ability. Thus, fraternal twins will be more genetically similar than if their parents were selected at random, and this will lead to the underestimation of the role of genetic factors and the over-estimation of the influence of the common environment on abilities.

Early behaviour-genetic studies were sometimes flawed for the reasons given above. However, methodologies have improved, and modern behaviour-genetic studies are much better designed, are based on large samples of individuals, ensure that adoptees are separated early and are genuinely reared apart, and take account of the problems raised by selective placement. They also provide remarkably consistent results. There is, of course, plenty more work to be done. Efforts are under way to actually measure the 'shared environment', to find out precisely which parts of it seem to influence children's cognitive ability. But this is harder than it seems, as Chipuer *et al.* (1993) found that people's *perceptions* of the family environment have a substantial genetic component! So asking people questions about their home environment will not provide an objective measure of the quality of that environment.

The 'nature–nurture debate' (as the study of genetic versus environmental factors is sometimes known) remains one of the most hotly debated and politically charged issues in psychology, with several other important issues surfacing periodically in the press and scientific journals. These include:

- the belief that because abilities have a substantial genetic component abilities cannot be changed. This ignores the finding that about 50 per cent of the variation in *g* is due to environmental influences.
- a concern that because genes are the most potent predictor of abilities within several cultural groups, differences in mean

levels of *g* between cultural or racial groups is also due to genetic effects: some races may be genetically 'inferior' to others. There is not a shred of evidence suggesting that any differences in *g* between racial/cultural groups are genetically mediated.

- concerns about the activities of the eugenics movement. Such groups argue that high levels of *g* within a society make it successful within a capitalist world-wide economy, *g* has a genetic component, and as there is a negative correlation between *g* and the number of children one has (Herrnstein and Murray, 1994) this will cause a gradual decline in levels of *g* within the society unless measures are taken to restrict breeding amongst low-IQ groups – a chilling prospect

- a more general suspicion that attributing *g* to the genes facilitates a right-wing agenda, rather than one that deals sympathetically with educational and environmental improvements for the disadvantaged. However, if genes had *no* effect on *g* then a child raised in an awful environment would have no chance whatsoever of excelling intellectually: genes serve to reduce the impact of poor or abusive environments.

- confusion about whether the heritability statistics discussed above refer to individuals or groups. It is wrong to conclude that because the shared environment has but a modest effect on levels of *g*, the family environment will not influence any children. It will influence some. It will not influence others. The 'modest' figure is an *average* within the population.

- the assumption that because the common environment has a small influence on *g*, extremely good (or unspeakably awful) family environments will have little effect on children's abilities. The heritability estimates given above are average figures, based on the sorts of environments that children typically experience in countries such as the United States, Sweden and the United Kingdom. Expose children to an environment quite unlike that experienced by others, and it is impossible to say what will happen.

Summary

Several different designs have been used to investigate the extent to which genetic makeup, a common environment and each individual's 'unique environment' influences a person's level of general ability. The results of family studies of twins, studies of separated siblings and twins (and their biological and adoptive parents) and other family studies not discussed above have shown a very consistent picture. Genetic makeup has the most potent influence on levels of general ability in western society (accounting for 50–60 per cent of the variation; rather less in childhood, and rather more in adulthood) followed by the common environment (important in childhood only) and the unique environment.

There is also a substantial literature that examines primary abilities rather than g and elementary cognitive tasks (e.g. Petrill et al., 1996), and physiological variables considered in Chapter 4, such as nerve conduction velocity and event-related potentials (e.g. Baker et al., 1991; Katsanis et al., 1997; Rijsdijk et al., 1995), and the search is under way to discover at the molecular level precisely which genes influence g – generally by comparing the genetic makeup of blood samples from high- and low-ability individuals (e.g. Plomin et al., 1995).

Whilst genetic studies show that the shared environment is an important determinant of children's general ability, they cannot reveal which particular aspects of home life matter. Research is under way to clarify this by directly measuring some aspects of the environment, for example by using the scale developed by Moos and Moos (1981) which assesses variables such as 'cohesion', 'conflict', 'expressiveness' and 'control' within the family. To complicate matters, it has been found that some aspects of the unique environment are under genetic control (Plomin et al., 1985). This sounds strange at first. However, it means that children whose genes predispose them to show high levels of general ability (given a suitable environment) are likely to modify their environment in order to develop their high ability. For example, they might join educational clubs at school, select highly intelligent peers as friends, take up intellectually demanding hobbies (e.g. chess) and so on. So far from being 'victims' of the environment, children may actually shape it to enhance their genetic potential.

The ubiquity of genetic influences on ability has one extremely important implication for many studies in social psychology and sociology. Suppose that a study is performed to link some aspect of parenting behaviour to children's performance. For example, we might study whether reading to 6 year olds is related to the children's verbal performance. The obvious research design would involve taking a sample of parents and estimating (through observation, interview or self-report) how many minutes the parents typically spend reading to their child in a week. This measure could then be correlated with the children's school performance (or, better, their language ability). If a substantial positive correlation were found, many researchers would infer that reading to children *causes* them to develop above-average verbal skill.

Of course, this is not necessarily the case. The simple environmental model discussed above is shown in Figure 4.1a: arrows indicate causal relations. So this suggests that parental reading behaviour causes children to develop good reading skills. However, it is also possible to propose a purely genetic model, shown in the middle of this figure. For as the parents are related to the children in this study, it is not the case that the parents' reading behaviour is the only influence on the children's verbal performance. The parents also pass over their genes. In the light of what has been said about the genetic basis of general ability, it is highly likely that possessing genes that are associated with high *g* may lead some parents to read to their children extensively, and for the children (who will inherit some of these genes) to develop good language skills. So it may not be the case that reading *causes* good verbal skills to develop. Both phenomena may be under genetic control, as shown in Figure 4.1b.

This model too is unrealistic, since it denies the possibility that the way in which parents behave towards their children can have *any* influence on their performance. Thus the model shown in Figure 4.1c is the most appropriate. This suggests that both

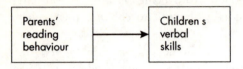

(a) environmental model

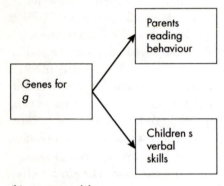

(b) genetic model

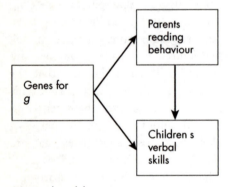

(c) mixed model

FIGURE 4.1 Three models to explain why a child may develop verbal skills (a) environmental model (b) genetic model (c) mixed model

the parents' genes and the behaviour of the parents (or adoptive parents) may influence the child's language ability. 'Genetically informed' research designs (for example, family/twin/adoption studies of the kind mentioned earlier) can be used to determine the relative importance of the environmental and genetic effects, and a number of studies (summarised in Thompson, 1993) suggest that genetic influences on the abilities of even young children are far too substantial to be ignored. Genetically naïve designs such as that shown in Figure 4.1a will confuse individual differences due to shared genes with those that result from the environment. They will overestimate the importance of the environment if an ability has any genetic component whatsoever. However, many psychologists are unaware of the literature discussed in this chapter (or were influenced by Kamin's post-hoc criticisms of some of the early studies) and so such studies are quite common in the literature. For example, is there *really* unequivocal evidence that smoking or drinking during pregnancy leads to lowered levels of general ability in the child?

As Mackintosh (1995) observed, recent evidence about the heritability of general ability 'has made an already pretty well established conclusion well-nigh irrefutable . . . no prudent person would now accept that the heritability of IQ was zero. That question is settled'. Snyderman and Rothman's (1987) survey of psychology academics also revealed that most academics now accept that general ability has a genetic component, and the American Psychological Association's *Task Force on Intelligence* reached much the same conclusion (Neisser *et al.*, 1996). All that remains is to identify the individual genes and their patterns of interaction.

Further reading

Bouchard, T.J. (1993) 'The genetic architecture of human intelligence' in P.A. Vernon (ed.) *Biological Approaches to the Study of Human Intelligence*, New York: Ablex. Good, modern acount of genetic and environmental influences on general ability.

Howe, M.J.A. (1998), 'Can IQ change?' *The Psychologist* 11: 69–72. An article stressing that although general ability has a strong genetic component, this does not imply that it is unchangeable.

Neisser, U., Boodoo, G., Bouchard, T., *et al.* (1996) 'Intelligence: knowns and unknowns', *American Psychologist* 51: 77–101. A list of accepted facts about general ability – including its genetic basis

Plomin, R. and Petrill, S.A. (1997) 'Genetics and intelligence: what's new?', *Intelligence* 24: 53–77. A brief summary of modern developments in the genetics of abilities, including molecular genetics, genetic influences on the environment, development aspects and the genetics of abilities other than *g*.

Rowe, D.C. (1997) 'A place at the policy table?' *Intelligence* 24: 133–158. Discusses the social implications of behaviour-genetic studies of abilities; for example, whether educators should focus on enhancing those abilities that have a substantial shared environmental component, and are thus more malleable than those with a very substantial genetic component.

Ability
processes

93

WHILST CHAPTERS 2 AND 3 spelt out in some detail what is known about the structure of individual differences, they said nothing about how or why they emerge. Why *do* some people have great difficulty visualising things or using numbers, for example? The results spelt out in Chapter 4 seem to suggest that at least part of the explanation may lie in biological processes, since general ability has a substantial genetic component, implying that some sorts of individual differences in the structure and/or functioning of the brain are likely to influence levels of general ability. This is certainly well established at the gross level: now that earlier measurement problems have been solved, it is known that individuals with larger brains tend to have above-average levels of general ability (Jensen and Sinha, 1993). Thus, there may be a place for some form of biological explanation.

However, it was also apparent from Chapter 4 that a purely biological model cannot be the sole explanation of individual differences in *g*. It seems to explain only 50–70 per cent of the observed variation in scores. So the search should also consider other factors, such as Sternberg's cognitive processes (described in Chapter 4), social processes, educational processes, and so on. The problem with studying these variables is that it is difficult to be sure which is cause and which effect. Does high *g* cause a child to read books, or does reading plenty of books boost *g*? It is very difficult ever to be sure. For this reason many researchers prefer instead to test some rather simple biological models. This chapter mainly focuses on biological models, but also considers the cognitive approaches of Sternberg and Hunt.

The speed of processing hypothesis

Many researchers in this area have concentrated on trying to explain general ability, or *g* – that is, developing an understanding of why scores on all ability tests (of very different kinds, some involving language and others not) are positively correlated together. One possible explanation for this is that some individuals are simply able to process information more quickly than others.

A facile example may help. Suppose that we took a random sample of computers, and measured how long it took each to perform various operations – such as drawing 1,000 coloured circles on the screen, performing a factor analysis of Thurstone's data, writing or reading a million characters to or from a file on its hard disc, rotating a standard 3-D image or using a particular algorithm to evaluate pi to 10,000 decimal places. Each of these tasks will depend for their speed on different parts of the computer. Some machines may have special graphics processors so that drawing circles and rotating images may be fast. Some may have disc drives that can access information unusually quickly: they will perform well when reading or writing to disc. Some may have processors that are designed to multiply and divide numbers rapidly, so they will perform the factor analysis and evaluate pi quickly.

If these six pieces of data were factor analysed, it is almost certain that one would find three factors: one corresponding to the efficiency of information transfer to and from the disc, another reflecting individual differences in the speed that the computer can manipulate images, and a third measuring its efficiency at performing numerical calculations. It is also certain that these three factors will be correlated together, as the speed with which the clock on the central processing unit ticks will affect *all* measures from a particular machine. We would therefore also find a single 'second-order factor'.

This hierarchical model has a passing resemblance to the structure of abilities described in Chapter 2: a set of relatively autonomous units (ability factors, or chunks of the computer) the speed of whose operation all depend to some extent on some other variable (*g*, or the speed with which the central processing unit runs). So one popular view regards general ability as a basic property of the nervous system that affects *all* cognitive operations that make up an individual performance. Jensen (1993) considers this sort of argument in some depth.

Two slightly different theories have emerged, but they are in most instances interchangeable, and so will be considered together. Several writers (Eysenck, 1967; Galton, 1883; Jensen and Munroe, 1974) have suggested that either the speed with which information is transmitted within or between neurones, or the *efficiency* of neural transmission, may be the key to *g*. Efficiency simply refers to how much information is lost when one nerve transits electrical impulses to another. So according to this model, high intelligence (*g*) should be associated with a brain that processes information quickly and accurately. It is difficult to envisage a simpler theory. But how might it be tested?

Direct measurement of neural conduction velocity

It is difficult to get access to neurones in the brain. However, if one makes the assumption that the same forces that influence speed/accuracy of information processing in the brain also influence peripheral nerves, then it is possible to test this hypothesis directly by:

(a) measuring an individual's general ability, using a test such as Raven's Matrices (Raven, 1965) or the Weschler Adult Intelligence Scale (Revised) (Weschler, 1974)

(b) applying two widely spaced electrodes to the skin above one of the nerves whose long axons run down the arm

(c) measuring the distance between these electrodes

(d) electrically stimulating the nerve by applying a small electric shock to one electrode

(e) timing how long it takes for the neural impulse to reach the other electrode

(f) repeating the process several times and averaging.

It is then possible to estimate the individual's neural conduction velocity by dividing the distance between the electrodes by the time delay between the application of the shock to one electrode and its arrival at the other, although the measures are somewhat variable and may be influenced by a number of physical variables, including temperature. Several studies have followed this pattern, some also correlating the neural conduction velocities (ncvs) with measures such as **inspection time** or reaction time (see p. 102). If the 'speed of neural conduction' hypothesis is correct, and it does not matter that a peripheral (rather than cerebral) nerve is chosen and that there is no synaptic transmission involved, then one would expect a positive correlation between ncv and g. Vernon and Mori (1992) did indeed find a significant correlation of 0.42–0.48 between ncv and g.

However, a number of studies have failed to replicate this finding (Barrett *et al.*, 1990; Reed and Jensen, 1991; Rijsdijk *et al.*, 1995; Wickett and Vernon, 1994) although these 'replications' also introduced some methodological differences, particularly with relation to temperature control. Curiously, the correlations in Vernon and Mori's data were much stronger for males than females. The reasons for this are not well understood (Wickett and Vernon, 1994). These results do not provide good evidence for the neuronal conduction model of g – though given the caveats mentioned above (peripheral versus central nerves, so differences in myelinisation; lack of synaptic transmission) such failures are not necessarily fatal for the theory either. But it may suggest that it is necessary to measure neural conduction velocity indirectly through experimental designs where the dependent variable is thought to be highly correlated with neural conduction velocity. The rest of this chapter examines some indirect measures of neural conduction velocity

Inspection time

Vickers, *et al.* (1972) developed a useful paradigm for estimating neural conduction velocity. They argued that as the retina is essentially an outgrowth of the brain, if the neural conduction velocity interpretation of *g* is correct, high-*g* individuals might be able to see/take-in/apprehend simple visual stimuli faster than low-*g* individuals. They developed a simple task, called inspection time, to measure how long it took individuals to see a simple image, and found that this did indeed have a substantial negative correlation with *g*, as expected.

The stimuli that they used are shown in Figure 5.1. Participants peer into a box (the tachistoscope). On a screen in front of them is a black dot on a white background. They push a button, and either the shape shown in Figure 5.1a or that in Figure 5.1b appears extremely briefly, and is immediately followed by the figure shown in Figure 5.1c, which stays on the screen for several seconds. Because of the short presentation times it is very difficult to see which of the two figures (5.1a or 5.1b) was presented. But for each trial participants are asked to say whether they believed that the left leg or the right leg of the stimulus was the longer. This procedure is repeated many more times, normally using at least thirty exposures at each of several durations. The experimenter then works out the percentage of correct answers at each duration, and from this estimates how long the stimulus has to be presented in order for a particular individual to have a particular probability (e.g. 90 per cent) of being able correctly

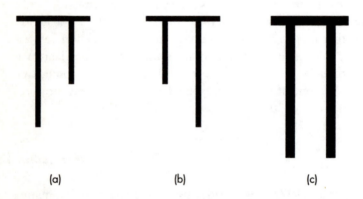

(a)   (b)   (c)

FIGURE 5.1 Two stimuli plus mask for an inspection-time task

to identify which of the two figures was presented. This is their *inspection time* (IT).

Nettelbeck and Lally (1976) suggested that the correlation between IT and general ability was approximately –0.9. Such a high correlation suggested that conventional tests of general ability could perhaps be replaced by this simple experimental technique. However, the reason why this correlation was so large is because the authors used participants who varied enormously in their levels of general ability: the sample comprised a sample of university students plus some individuals with moderate to severe learning difficulties, and all of these people showed very long inspection times and very low scores on the test of general ability. The experiment has been repeated a great many times using better samples of people, however, and several good reviews of these findings have been published (e.g. Deary, 1997; Deary and Stough, 1996; Kranzler and Jensen, 1989; Nettelbeck, 1987). The correlation between IT and general ability seems to be in the order of –0.4 to –0.55, with Kranzler and Jensen's meta-analysis concluding that best estimate for the correlation is –0.54. Thus it is probably fair to say that about a quarter (-0.54^2) of the variability in g can be explained by IT. The correlation is generally rather higher for tests measuring Gf than those with a verbal component Gc, and at the level of primary abilities, IT correlates best with perceptual speed (Cooper *et al.*, 1986).

Other methods of measuring IT have been developed. These include changing the rate at which a light flashes to determine the point where an individual can just detect whether it is flickering or lit continuously (Nettelbeck, 1982), and a tactile version in which a person is invited to place two fingers on two metal plates. The plates are then made to vibrate, one marginally before the other, and the participant is invited to say which finger was stimulated first;. It does not correlate very well with measures of ability (Nettelbeck and Kirby, 1983). An effective auditory form has been developed (Deary *et al.*, 1989) where two briefly presented tones differ in pitch. Inspection time here is the duration necessary for the pitch-difference to be reliably detected.

The whole point of IT studies is that they supposedly measure a very simple aspect of individual differences – the amount of time needed to interpret a very simple pattern that is projected on the retina. It has deliberately been designed to be as simple as possible so that no meta-components (strategies) should be able to influence performance on this task. For if it is found that it is possible to devise strategies to improve performance, then IT loses its theoretical appeal as an experimental measure of how long a person's nervous system takes to process a standard stimulus: the task becomes of little interest.

It has been claimed that scores on an IT task *can* be influenced by perceptual strategies, such as looking for flicker at the ends of the legs (Alexander and Mackenzie, 1992): the correlations between inspection time and g might thus arise because individuals with high g notice certain cues that make the task easier. However, this strategy cannot explain the correlation between inspection time and ability (Chaiken and Young, 1993; Egan, 1994) as there is a relationship between IT and g for both cue-users and non-cue-users. The outer parts of the retina are more sensitive to flicker than the central fovea, and so the 'flickering light' measure of IT becomes easier if individuals take advantage of this and look at the flickering lights out of the corner of their eyes. Or perhaps low-ability individuals will be less likely to concentrate hard throughout a gruelling bout of testing: a high error-rate will be interpreted as a slow inspection time. Perhaps practice is important: this could present problems if some of the high-ability participants (typically psychology students) are more used to taking part in cognitive experiments than are others. There is not space to discuss such issues in detail, and in any case Brody (1992: 68–71) gives a good account of these problems, whilst White's (1996) and Levy's (1992) articles contain a useful discussion of how the IT paradigm fits in to modern theories of cognitive psychology and psychophysics. Deary's (1997; Deary and Stough, 1996) reviews are also useful.

So is the correlation between inspection time

● well-established fact

- likely to be due to some fairly basic neural processes
- large enough to be important?

The first point is not really in dispute: a wide range of inspection-time paradigms have been correlated with scores on many different ability tests in many different samples (ranging from young children to elderly people) world-wide, with a surprising unanimity of results: there really does seem to be a consistent correlation of about −0.5 between IT and general ability.

There is no direct evidence to answer the second point. None of the experiments performed to measure neural conduction velocity seem to have included an inspection-time task. Had they done so, it would be possible to directly correlate IT with ncv, in order to check whether there is substantial overlap between these two measures. Do the same neural processes that are measured in the inspection-time task actually *cause* individual differences in ability, are they consequences of such individual differences, or are both influenced by some other variables? To answer this, Deary (1995) measured inspection time and general ability on two occasions, two years apart, in a sample of schoolchildren. His analysis allowed him to test whether the children's ability levels at age 11 determined their IT performance at age 13, whether their IT at 11 determined their levels of ability at 13, or whether the relationship was not causal. The second model fitted the data best, suggesting that individual differences in IT are likely to *cause* individual differences in general ability.

Finally, are the correlations between inspection-time and ability large enough to bother about? Howe (1997) writes: 'The correlations are found to be relatively low, typically around + .3 to + .4 or less,[1] which means that they "account for" up to about 15 per cent of the variability in people's scores'. It is clear that he does not regard such correlations (which are also somewhat lower than the generally agreed estimates mentioned above) as particularly substantial. However, when one considers all the other variables that might influence general ability, finding

---

[1] Presumably should read '−0.3 to −0.4'.

one simple task that seems able to explain about 15 per cent (Howe's figure) to 30 per cent (Kranzler and Jensen, 1989) of the variation certainly seems to be a useful step forward. Statistical rules of thumb have, in any case, been developed to assess the 'effect size'. Here a population correlation of 0.5 is conventionally regarded as a 'large effect' and one of 0.3 a 'medium effect' (Cohen, 1988): Howe's assertion that correlations between inspection time and general ability are 'relatively low' is thus surprising.

Reaction time and g

If there are individual differences in the speed with which people's neurones process information, how else might this show itself? The inspection-time task discussed above focused on the amount of time it took to perceive a stimulus. It should also be possible to measure the amount of time taken to respond to a stimulus – a measure known as reaction time. In the simplest possible reaction-time task, a person may be given a button to hold, and asked to wait for some event (e.g. a light being turned on): when this happens the person is instructed to press the button as quickly as possible. The delay between the onset of the light and the start of the response is known as the 'simple reaction time'. In a typical experiment, an individual's reaction time would be measured forty or fifty times, then averaged. It is also possible to calculate the variability of each person's reaction times, which shows how consistent the person's reaction times are.

It is also possible to devise more complicated tasks. A **choice reaction time** apparatus used by Arthur Jensen is shown diagramatically in Figure 5.2. Eight electric push-buttons have lights mounted on their tops, rather like those found on gaming machines. These are arranged equidistant from a ninth button, the 'home button', as shown in Figure 5.2. All eight lights are switched off, and participants are invited to hold down the home button with the index finger of their preferred hand. After a variable-length pause (typically one to three seconds) one of the eight buttons is illuminated; the participant is asked to lift the finger

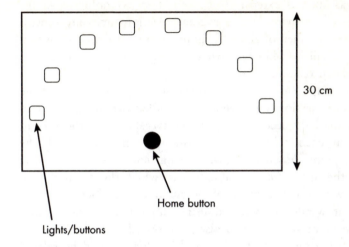

FIGURE 5.2 Jensen's choice reaction-time apparatus

from the home button and press the illuminated button as quickly as possible. Two measures are calculated from this experiment:

- the time that elapses between the button being illuminated and the participant lifting the finger from the home button ('reaction time' or 'RT')
- the time that elapses between lifting the finger from the home button and pressing the illuminated button ('movement time' or 'MT').

As before, this procedure is performed many times, and the individual's mean reaction time, mean movement time (and their variabilities) are calculated – normally after 'cleaning up' the data a little to ignore any trials where the RT or MT was very long or very short, suggesting a lapse of attention or a lucky attempt at predicting when and which button would be illuminated.

The procedure is then repeated using the same participant after masking off some of the lights using metal plates, so that only one, two or four (adjacent) lights are visible. It is well known that people's reaction time becomes longer as the number of lights to be scanned increases – a phenomenon known as 'Hick's Law', which was studied extensively by cognitive psychologists in the 1960s. So if the participant's average reaction times are plotted against the number of lights, a graph similar to that shown in Figure 5.3 will be obtained, where a line is drawn through the various mean reaction times.

This graph shows two important things. The height of the line shows how slowly the person responded overall: if a second person took 0.05 seconds longer (on average) than the first to respond in each condition, then that person's line would be parallel to that shown in Figure 5.3, but somewhat higher. The slope of the line indicates the extent to which the reaction time slows down as the number of potential targets increases. The experiment would be repeated using other participants, whose level of general ability would also be assessed.

Both the height of the line and its slope should be related to general ability. The reaction-time task is likely to involve two stages. The first involves scanning the lights, noticing which has come on, and deciding which way the finger should move. The second step involves actually initiating the movement.

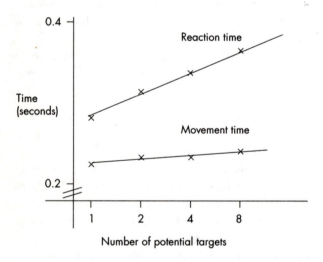

FIGURE 5.3 One individual's reaction time and movement time as a function of targets in a choice reaction time

We know from cognitive psychology that increasing the number of targets leads to longer reaction times. This implies that more cognitive processing (of some kind) is involved when carrying out a four-choice reaction-time task than when carrying out a two- or one-choice task. Imagine that two people, Maud and Claude, sat the reaction-time task described above. Suppose too that Claude's nervous system takes twice as long to processes information as Maud's. We would expect their lines to be of different heights, as Claude takes longer to initiate the response than does Maud. We would also expect the lines to differ in slope if Claude takes twice as long (rather than a fixed amount longer) to scan the various lights, notice that one has lit up, and decide which way the finger should move. Claude's line will slope more steeply than Maud's, as shown in Figure 5.4. So we might expect both the height of the line (its *intercept*) and its slope to have a negative correlation with general ability.

Several such studies have been performed, the early ones being summarised by Jensen (1987). They generally support this

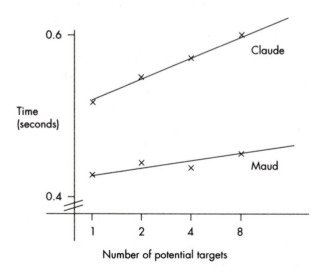

FIGURE 5.4 Hypothetical reaction times of two individuals differing in neural processing speed

hypothesis – but although correlations between g and the slope or height of the line are usually statistically significant, they are not large (about –0.2). One of the problems with reaction-time studies is that they confuse speed with consistency of performance. Rapid mean reaction times can be obtained only when individuals (a) respond quickly, and (b) respond *consistently* fast. If participants in the reaction-time experiment sometimes day-dream or let their attention wander, then this may lead to some very long response times. Thus it is unsurprising to find that the standard deviation of people's response times is also related to g. Participants with high scores on general ability tests perform both rapidly and consistently at the reaction-time task (e.g. Barrett *et al.*, 1986).

Other tasks may also be used to measure reaction time: the 'odd man out' paradigm (Frearson and Eysenck, 1986) uses Jensen's apparatus, but instead of just one light being illuminated, three come on together. Two of these are close to each other and another is further away. The participant is asked to push the illuminated button that is furthest from the other two. Reaction times from this task correlate about –0.48 to –0.62 with general ability (Frearson and Eysenck, 1986; Frearson *et al.*, 1988) – somewhat higher than Jensen's measures. And when several different measures of reaction time are used to predict general ability (using a technique known as multiple regression), the reaction-time measures can explain between 10 per cent and 50 per cent of the variation in g within the samples of people tested (Vernon, 1990).

As with inspection time, it is necessary to consider whether the correlation between general ability and reaction times is

- well established
- likely to be caused by basic neural processes
- large enough to be interesting.

The correlation between reaction time and g has been found often enough in the literature to make it a 'safe' phenomenon, albeit not the largest one known to humankind. Jensen (1993) talks about and tries to explain the '–0.35 barrier', since it is rather difficult to find reaction-time measures that correlate better than this with measures of g.

The second issue is more vexed: that is, whether reaction times really do measure simple speed-of-processing. True, Vernon and Mori (1992) did find a significant correlation between nerve conduction velocity and g, but given the problems in replicating the ncv/g correlation, it is probably unwise to make too much of this. There have also been some methodological criticisms of Jensen's work (Longstreth, 1984, 1986). For example:

- Jensen began by measuring RTs to one light, then two, four and eight of them, rather than varying the order in which the conditions were administered, and when Widaman and Carlson (1989) gave the eight-light trials first and then worked their way down to the one-light trials, they found a *positive* correlation between slope and g! However, this criticism cannot apply to the simple (one-choice) reaction-time data, which still shows a correlation of about –0.19 with g (Jensen, 1987).

- Detterman and Daniel (1989) and Rabbitt (1985) argue that the reaction-time task is far from being a simple measure of processing speed, but may instead involve a number of cognitive strategies – for example, in deciding which error rate is acceptable when performing the task. Some individuals may respond very rapidly but may often push the wrong button; others may respond slowly but make no errors. Perhaps high g individuals respond rapidly but make many errors? However, this is not the case: high-g individuals make *fewer* errors than others (Jensen, 1987).

- The Jensen task is quite gruelling, and participants need to concentrate hard throughout in order to achieve fast average reaction times, or RTs that show a small standard deviation. High-ability individuals may be better able to concentrate, and perhaps *this* is the real reason why some people tend to perform rather well on both tests? Larson and Alderton (1990) found evidence supporting this idea, as an individual's worst reaction time (probably indicating a lapse of attention) was a better predictor of *g* than the fastest reaction time.

● It is found that the response that is made following an error in a reaction-time task is rather slower than normal and that participants who have very low scores on ability tests tend to slow down much more than others following a mistake on a reaction-time task (Brewer and Smith, 1984). So perhaps this strategy explains the differences in mean scores? (Brody, 1992: 59 argues that it cannot.)

There seems to be a very real possibility that individual differences noted in the reaction-time tasks may correlate with *g* because individuals high on general ability are more able than others to perform at a consistent level of performance. Although measures of reaction time do consistently show correlations with *g*, such correlations are both fairly modest in size, and may well reflect individual differences in attention rather than pure mental speed.

Finally, is the link between RT and *g* large enough to be interesting? Perhaps – but the relationships are generally rather small, and individual differences in strategy-use and attention may well complicate the relationship. More researchers now focus on inspection time, where the correlations are larger and the confounding variables fewer.

What are the practical implications of individual differences in reaction time? Once again, if a task requires someone to choose quickly and consistently between several different responses, high *g* is likely to facilitate performance of this task. So there may well be a correlation between *g* and scores on arcade games of the 'shoot'em-up' variety. Whether this is due to the direct influence of *g* or the effect of concentration is another matter.

Physiological correlates of *g*

If tests measuring general ability, *g*, reflect some aspects of activity in the nervous system (as suggested by behaviour-genetic studies, and work on inspection time and reaction time considered above) rather than a mere convenient description of the way in which we behave (Howe, 1988b), then we might expect to find some links between scores on tests of *g* and various physiological measures of brain activity. Some of these use electrodes fixed to the scalp to measure electrical activity in the brain (the **electro-encephalogram** or **EEG**). Some do so following some sort of stimulation (**evoked potential recordings**). Yet others use **positron emission tomography** (**PET scans**) to show which areas of the brain are most active whilst people are solving various sorts of problems, and so link both the extent and location of neural activity to *g*.

General ability and the electroencephalogram (EEG)

As Deary and Carryl (1993) observe, 'the enterprise was begun on little more than the premise that, since IQ tests and EEG traces both have something to do with g and brain functioning, then aspects of the latter might correlate with the former.' Attempts to discover which (if any) of the various aspects of the EEG are linked to general ability continue apace, with some important but complex theories emerging – e.g. the work of Hendrickson (1982a), Robinson (1996) and Weiss (1986, 1989).

Measuring the EEG involves attaching a dozen or two electrodes to a set of standard locations on the scalp. These electrodes pick up electrical activity from various parts of the brain, and each is connected to a highly sensitive amplifier, and thence to a computer to allow the electrical activity to be recorded and analysed. It is found that the level of electrical activity at a particular electrode often rises and falls in a regular manner over time. For example, it may be found that the voltage 'peaks' every 0.1 second or so. It is possible to analyse the pattern of electrical activity from an electrode, and work out how long there is between each peak – the frequency of the EEG. One of the most important types of brain activity is **alpha activity**. This corresponds to large swings in electrical activity that peak between eight and thirteen times every second (8–13 Hz) and is found when the person being tested is relaxed and awake.

So are individual differences in the EEG related to abilities? EEGs have been recorded from participants when doing nothing or performing some mental activity (e.g. solving multiplication problems). Various investigators have focused on different electrodes, and scrutinised different bands of EEG frequencies (some would look at activity in the whole alpha range of 8–13 Hz, whilst others focus on much narrower ranges of frequencies).

There is one good reason for *not* expecting any statistics derived from the EEG to correlate substantially with *g*: it has been found that the same individual can produce rather different results when tested on a different occasion and/or in a different setting (O'Gorman and Lloyd, 1985) for reasons that are not well understood. This will result in low or inconsistent correlations between EEG measures and anything else. However, some consistent findings did emerge from Deary and Carryl's (1993) excellent review, on which I have drawn extensively below. For example, Giannitrapani (1985) measured 100 children's EEG whilst performing various tasks, and at rest. He found that the extent to which the children showed electrical activity of exactly thirteen cycles per second correlated substantially ($r > 0.4$) and significantly with general ability. Other adjacent frequencies (e.g. 11 Hz) showed no such relationships. Other studies have focused on the whole band of alpha frequencies, and once again children and adults who show most alpha activity tend to perform better at tests of general ability (e.g. Gasser *et al.*, 1983; Giannitrapani, 1969; Mundy-Castle, 1958). These correlations can be quite substantial (in the order of 0.4–0.5) and some of these also found correlations between other frequency bands and general ability. As Deary and Caryl (1993: 264) note, substantial correlations such as this 'allow us to dismiss as uninformed authors such as Howe (1988a, 1988b) who have questioned whether *any* biological measures can be found which correlate with *g* once studies involving retarded subjects have been excluded'.

General ability and average evoked potentials (AEPs)

Evoked potential recordings examine the pattern of electrical activity at just one site of the brain following some form of sensory stimulation. This is often a tone or click presented via headphones or a flash of light, and the experiment is usually repeated 100 or so times and the results averaged (hence 'average evoked potential'). In essence, this approach examines how long it takes the individual's brain to react to the auditory stimuli. When the AEPs of a number of people are examined, the graphs generally have a similar shape. Immediately after presenting the tone, nothing happens for a few tenths of a second, and then a pattern of peaks and troughs emerges.

The various peaks and troughs have been given names, such as P-300. So it is easy to measure how long after the stimulus is presented each of these parts of the waveform is found. Individual differences in the amount of time between the stimulus being presented and one of the characteristics of the AEP appearing can be measured, and correlated with the participants' levels of general ability. Several of the studies reviewed by Deary and Carryl (1993) and Stelmack and Houlihan (1995) report a negative correlation between general ability and the amount of time that elapses before various features of the AEP waveform are seen: that is, high levels of general ability are associated with rapid processing of information (e.g. Ertl and Schafer, 1969). However, there are also several studies that fail to find such relationships (e.g. Barrett and Eysenck, 1992; Rust, 1975) and some that find *positive* correlations! Most of the findings are non-significant, however, and so it is probably safe to conclude that individual differences in the time that it takes various parts of the AEP waveform to appear owe nothing to general ability. Likewise, whilst some researchers find that the *height* of the AEP waveform is positively correlated with general ability (e.g. Haier *et al.*, 1983), once again there are many notable failures to replicate this effect (e.g. Barrett and Eysenck; 1992; Rust, 1975). It also used to be thought that the 'spikiness' of the AEP was also related to *g* (Hendrickson, 1982a, 1982b) but this effect has proved difficult to replicate (Barrett and Eysenck, 1992).

General ability and positron emission tomography (PET) scans

It is now possible to determine which parts of the brain are active when an individual is performing cognitive tasks. Brain cells metabolise glucose; the more neural activity that takes place at a certain location in the brain, the more glucose it uses. So the problem is to find some way of determining how rapidly various parts of the brain are using glucose whilst an individual performs various types of mental activity. The rate of glucose metabolism at various locations may then be related to *g* or other abilities.

If radioactive glucose is injected into a volunteer's arm, it is possible to detect this radiation in the brain once the radioactive glucose begins to be metabolised. The more active the neurones in a particular area, the more glucose they will burn up – and so the more radioactive they will become. This is the basis of positron emission tomography studies of neural functioning. It has been found that there are substantial individual differences in the extent to which individuals metabolise (radioactive) glucose whilst solving difficult abstract reasoning tasks, and there are very substantial negative correlations (in the order of –0.7 to –0.8) between the amount of glucose metabolised and *g* (Haier *et al.*, 1988). People with high levels of general ability seem to have brains that are more efficient, in that they use less glucose when solving problems than do those low in *g*. This study was based on a sample of only eight participants, but other independent studies have found much the same finding with larger samples (e.g. Parks *et al.*, 1988). Further studies have explored the role of practice. Do highly intelligent individuals show a greater drop in neural activity when they learn to perform a complex task? Haier *et al.* (1992) carried out PET scans twice (four weeks apart) on a sample of individuals who were learning to play a computer-game. Sure enough, the participants with highest levels of general ability showed the greatest decline in glucose metabolism (e.g. greatest efficiency). However, one study found the opposite effect, for reasons that are not at all well understood (Larson *et al.*, 1995).

Componential analysis

Are purely cognitive approaches any more useful for understanding the processes underpinning g (and other abilities) than the biological models considered thus far? Prior to developing his triarchic theory, Sternberg (1977) built on the work of Carroll (1980, 1983) which tried to understand the cognitive processes that went on when a person solved a single item in an intelligence test. The basic idea is very simple. The first step is to determine (through a process of logic, experiment or by interviewing participants) what sequence of cognitive operations is performed when solving a particular problem – developing a flowchart that shows precisely which mental operations are performed in which order to solve a particular problem. Next we make the assumption that each of the processes shown in the flowchart takes an individual a particular amount of time to perform. For example, it might take one individual 0.15 seconds to retrieve the meaning of a word (of a particular length and frequency of usage) from memory, whilst it may take someone else only 0.10 seconds to perform this operation. So the second step involves designing and carrying out experiments to measure how long individuals take to perform each of these 'elementary cognitive operations' (ECOs). Once we establish this, the third step involves inserting all the various times in the flowchart and thus making a prediction about how long it will take an individual to solve this particular test item. This prediction can be compared with the amount of time that it actually takes them to correctly solve this problem, and so the predictive power of the model can be determined.

This approach tries to understand what goes on when people solve individual items in a test. However, it is not in any way incompatible with the models of ability discussed in Chapter 2 or 3: it is quite possible that primary factors, second-order factors and g would be reflected in the correlations between various cognitive processes. For example, some individuals may be fast at performing all ECOs involving language, which would translate into high verbal ability. Or some individuals may be faster than others at performing all ECOs – giving g.

One of Sternberg's (1977) experiments involved cartoon characters. Like those shown in Figure 5. 5, these characters could vary in gender, tubbiness, height and shading, with two levels of each of these factors. Thus there were a total of sixteen of these 'people-piece' characters. Groups of four of these characters were shown to participants, and used to represent an analogy task, rather as shown in Figure 5.5. The participant is asked to infer the rule that links the second character to the first (in this example the sex differs, whilst height, tubbiness and shading are the same). The person then applies this rule to the third character (here a short, thin unshaded man) and can infer that if the analogy is true, the fourth character must therefore be a short, thin unshaded woman. They compare this with the *actual* fourth character, notice that the fourth character is not the one that was expected, and so conclude that the analogy is false.

Thus in Sternberg's experiment, participants are given two buttons to press – one if the analogy shown to them is true, and the other if it is false. Then they are shown various problems, and asked to decide whether each is true or false, reacting as quickly as possible.

The really clever part of this experiment is this. Sometimes, the participant is shown the leftmost one, two or three figures for several seconds before the clock starts and the rest of the characters appear. This allows the participant to solve part of the problem in advance; for example, if the first two characters are

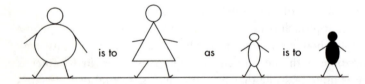

FIGURE 5.5 Example of a schematic analogy task, reading: 'Tall fat unshaded man is to tall fat unshaded woman as short thin unshaded man is to short, thin, shaded man' – an incorrect analogy. If correct the fourth character would show a short, thin, unshaded woman

shown, the participant can work out in advance precisely which rule must be applied to the third figure when it appears. If the leftmost three figures are shown, the participant can work out what the correct answer should be, and merely has to check whether or not the final figure is correct. Without going into details, this allows Sternberg to estimate how long it takes *each individual participant* to perform each of six 'elementary cognitive operations', under a particular model. These are

- *encoding*, i.e. recognising each feature of the cartoon characters
- *inference*, i.e. noting which features changed between the first pair of characters, thus inferring the rule to be applied to the second pair of characters
- *mapping* the relation between the first and third characters
- *applying* the rule to the third character
- *comparing* the fourth character to what it should be
- *responding* appropriately.

The problem is that even for a simple task such as this, the number of possible models for solving it becomes very large, and it seems that participants use different metacomponents (e.g. initially scanning to see whether any of the characters is of a different height, colour, tubbiness or gender from the other three, in which case the analogy must be false) and that some of the operations may be performed in parallel. For example, it is possible that some individuals may simultaneously encode all four salient features of the characters. So different individuals may go about solving the problem in quite different ways, and it is difficult to test all possible competing models.

One of the early hopes of this approach was that once the durations of an individual's ECOs were known (from the people-piece task), it should be possible to predict rather accurately how long it would take that person to solve other problems that involved some or all of these ECOs. For example, if a quite different problem is thought to involve three encoding operations plus one inference and a response, then it should be possible to 'plug in' the durations estimated from the people-piece task and estimate how long it will take an individual to solve this new problem. Unfortunately this does not always seem to work well in practice (e.g. May *et al.*, 1987; Sternberg and Gardner, 1983).

Hunt's work on verbal ability

Sternberg's work is important as it attempts to determine how many independent cognitive operations are performed when people solve rather complex tasks, and to estimate the duration of each of them for a particular person. There is also a substantial literature that has selectively focused on some cognitive processes. We shall just mention one approach – that of E. B. Hunt – to give a flavour of the sorts of experiments that have been performed. Hunt was interested in individual differences in verbal ability, and how these related to memory process. He believed that speed of lexical access may be the key to understanding these individual differences. Perhaps some individuals are better able than others to retrieve the meanings of letters from memory. So Hunt (1978) asked participants to each perform two experiments. In one, they were shown pairs of letters, and were asked to decide whether the two letters in each pair were physically identical (aa; BB) rather than different (ab; Aa) by pressing one button if a pair was identical, and another button if they were physically different. Their reaction times were recorded.

The same participants then took part in a second experiment that involved exactly the same pairs of letters. However, they were now asked to press one button if the letter pairs referred to the same letter of the alphabet (Aa; bB) or not (Ab; bA). The mean time that it took participants to recognise that a pair of letters was physically identical was then subtracted from the average time that it took them to recognise that the two letters referred to the same letter of the alphabet. This was thought to reflect the amount of time that it took to retrieve the meaning of the letter from memory – the speed of lexical access. So does speed of lexical access predict verbal ability? Unfortunately, although statistically significant, the link is not as strong as Hunt had expected; it has consistently been found that the correlation is in the order of –0.3 (Hunt, 1978). Thus, although speed of lexical access does seem to be an important component of verbal ability, other cognitive processes must also be involved. Carroll (1993: 478–480) briefly summarises some other tasks that have been used to measure other mental processes. Here too correlations above 0.3 with abilities are rarely found.

Summary

This chapter has reviewed much evidence concerning the neural and cognitive correlates of abilities. Although experiments relating direct measures of neural conduction velocity to g have yielded inconsistent results, indirect methods of estimating neural conduction velocity such as inspection time (and, to a lesser extent, reaction time) do provide some support for the 'speed of information processing' view of general ability. The evidence from the physiological studies is harder to interpret. Studies of the resting EEG do seem to show a consistent relationship between some aspects of brain electrical activity and general ability. There also seems to be a link between g and efficiency of neural processing (as measured by PET scans). What is lacking are testable theories that explain why alpha activity *should* be related to g, and why some individuals metabolise less glucose when performing mental tasks than do others.

There is some suggestion that the speed of performing some cognitive operations (e.g. lexical access) is related to general ability. However, the correlations are too small to suggest that the ability factors *just* reflect individual differences in the speed of these operations. Sternberg's work tried to establish which cognitive processes individuals performed when carrying out simple cognitive tasks, the order in which they performed them, and the amount of time it took an individual to perform each of them. In practice the number of possible ways of performing even apparently simple tasks becomes enormous, and it becomes impossible to choose between several competing models which provide almost equally good fit to the data.

One term that has cropped up throughout this chapter is 'attention' (Posner, 1980). It is believed to be important in reaction-time and inspection-time studies (where lapses of attention lead to longer estimates), the EEG (where it is reflected in high levels of alpha activity), and in the sorts of problems studied by both the cognitive psychologists and by brain imagers, where the instructions will invariably ask participants to attend closely to the task. It should surely be incorporated into any new theory that links abilities to neural functioning.

There are several reasons why it important to try to understand the processes that underpin ability factors. In science, identifying structures or regularities are just the first step towards understanding a phenomenon. A bird-watcher who can distinguish between hundreds of species is not an expert biologist. An alchemist who can reliably cause impressive explosions on mixing certain substances is not a chemist. Science is all about developing and testing models about how and why things work – and in the case of individual differences, this means trying to understand why and how different people show different levels of various abilities. This is the most fundamental reason why it is important to try to 'look inside the black box', or develop an understanding of how abilities operate.

The second reason why such research is important is that links between g and inspection time, reaction time, the EEG and glucose metabolism suggests that this ability factor reflects to some neural processes – rather as suggested by the genetic studies discussed in Chapter 4. This runs counter to Howe's (1997: 30) claim that 'there are no convincing reasons at all for insisting that g is something real' and his disagreement with Herrnstein and Murray's (1994: 29) assertion that g is 'more than an artifact of statistical manipulation'. If g were just a statistical artifact, if could have no correlations with anything. These studies also show that factor analysis *can* identify low-level causal influences on performance, much as proposed in Chapter 2, suggesting that this statistical technique cannot be quite as useless as some critics (e.g. Gould, 1996) suggest.

Finally, there may be practical applications: to select someone who can perform simple visual discriminations or who can make perceptual decisions very quickly (e.g. in an aeroplane emergency) it may be worthwhile selecting for high g. If drugs are found that can speed neural conduction, could these perhaps increase g? So although there is an urgent need for a comprehensive theory to integrate all our knowledge about intelligence and brain function, this is a promising route to understanding how abilities originate and operate.

Further reading

Anderson, M. (1992) *Intelligence and Development*, Oxford: Blackwell. Chapter 3 is useful and thoughtful, though now slightly dated.

Deary, I.J. (1997) 'Intelligence and information processing', in H. Nyborg (ed.) *The Scientific Study of Human Nature*, Oxford: Pergamon. An excellent overview.

Jensen, A.R. (1998) *The g Factor*, New York: Praeger. Chapters 6 and 8 are highly readable, if somewhat detailed.

Matthews, G. and Dorn, L. (1995) 'Cognitive and attentional processes in personality and intelligence', in D.H. Saklofske and M. Zeidner (eds) *International Handbook of Personality and Intelligence*, New York: Plenum. For those with a background in cognitive psychology who are interested in a wider range of phenomena than are covered in this chapter. Readers may want to ignore the 'extroversion' sections.

Correlates of abilities

THE PREVIOUS CHAPTERS OF this book have been largely theoretical; they have examined statistical models of the structure of abilities, and some of the processes that may explain why, precisely, some individuals show different patterns of abilities from others. This chapter is much more applied in orientation. First, it considers the role of ability tests in applied psychology (particularly personnel selection) where many employers find that the routine psychometric testing of applicants makes a cost-effective and generally fair contribution to selection batteries that are designed to ensure that the applicants with the greatest potential are identified and appointed.

The second part of this chapter examines an attempt to find out what, precisely, the social implications of having high (or low) general ability are in modern-day American society. In other words, what the practical implications of scores on ability tests? What sorts of lives do high- and low- ability students lead once they leave school or college? Does society reward g? Is social class much more important than g in determining an individual's eventual place in society? In 1994 a book, *The Bell Curve* (Herrnstein and Murray, 1994), generated considerable controversy because it suggested that g is a potent predictor of success in twentieth-century America. Its authors claimed that children's level of general ability is likely to predict not only their subsequent academic performance and income, but also their likelihood of becoming dependent on welfare benefits, having large numbers of children, committing crime, etc. – variables that have more often been linked to social class than to g. Herrnstein and Murray examined the influence of social factors as well as g, and concluded that social background is a worse predictor of these variables than is g. And since g may have a substantial genetic basis and is arguably difficult to change substantially through training programmes or interventions, it has been claimed that this model suggests that there may be a permanent underclass in American society.

Ability tests in applied psychology

Ability tests are big business. Many businesses and other organisations have found that ability tests provide a cost-effective means of selecting employees, identifying individuals who might most benefit from a training course, and so on. And so a great number of tests have been developed for this purpose. They are generally used following some sort of job analysis (for instance involving interviews with current employees to determine the skills that are necessary for the post, or where an occupational psychologist will 'shadow' an employee and note what they do).

Four main types of ability tests have been developed for use in personnel selection and placement: individual tests of ability, group tests, performance tests and work-samples.

Individual tests of ability

These tests tend to be both comprehensive (i.e. they measure a wide range of abilities) and precise (i.e. the scores closely approximate candidates' true levels of ability). Individual tests of ability have been developed for both adults and children of various ages. One of the best known series of tests was developed by David Weschler, who was a clinical psychologist at Bellvue Hospital, New York, during the 1930s. The Weschler Adult Intelligence Scale (WAIS) is for ages 16+, the Weschler Intelligence Scale for Children (WISC) for those aged 6–16, and the Weschler Primary and Preschool Scale of Intelligence (WPPSI) for those aged 4–6½. Each measures a dozen or so abilities, which are conventionally divided into two sets of tests: verbal and performance. The verbal tests include those enquiring about information (e.g. 'who was George Washington?'), comprehension ('why do people wear clothes?'), similarities ('in what way are relay-races, tables and people alike?'), vocabulary ('what is an aardvark?'), arithmetic ('if a tin of beans costs 45p, how much will seven of them cost?') and a test called digit span where the participant is asked to repeat strings of numbers read aloud by the examiner (e.g. '1 3 3 2 5 4 7 8 4 9 1'). Performance tests involve solving jigsaws (where the solution time is noted), arranging blocks into specified patterns, noticing what feature is missing from a picture (e.g. a dog with an ear missing), arranging a series of 'cartoon-strip' style pictures so that they tell a logical story (e.g. boy kicks football/ball breaks window/man shouts behind broken window) and coding (e.g. 'if A = *, B = +, C = $, D = !, what does $ * + spell?').

From these tests it is possible to estimate people's overall IQ, their verbal or performance IQ, or their performance on the individual sub-tests.[1] There are other individual tests, too, such as the Stanford-Binet and the British Ability Scales. However, all of these scales take a long time to complete (generally at least an hour), can be used only with individuals and so tend not to be used for selection purposes unless a very accurate measure of ability is required. A second major problem with the Weschler tests is that they simply fail to measure all of the abilities described in Chapter 2 and 3, as they are not tied to any modern theory of ability. For example, there is nothing measuring any form of creativity, so the Gr factor cannot emerge. Digit span is the only memory test. And some of the measures (e.g. information) are likely to be culture-dependent. There are also real problems about the factor structure of the WISC, which seems to measure four second-order factors, not the two (verbal and non-verbal intelligence) conventionally interpreted (Cooper, 1995).

---

[1] IQ, or 'intelligence quotient', is simply a normally distributed scale having a mean of 100 and a standard deviation of (usually) 15. This means that it is easy to work out how an individual's score relates to others of the same age. For example, if a child has an IQ of 130 (or two standard deviations above the mean) tables of the normal distribution function show that only 2.5% of children have scores above this value.

Group tests of ability are much more popular in applied psychology. These tests are printed in booklets, and so one examiner can simultaneously test twenty or more people, which makes large-scale screening a practical proposition. Some tests, such as Raven's Matrices (Raven, 1965), just measure general reasoning ability through abstract problems rather like that shown in Figure 6.1. Others measure a whole range of primary abilities (Bennett *et al.*, 1978; Ekstrom *et al.*, 1976; Hakstian and Cattell, 1976; United States Employment Service, 1979). Yet others measure several abilities that may correspond to some of the primary or secondary abilities discussed in Chapter 2 (e.g. Heim *et al.*, 1970). For the purposes of personnel selection, there rarely seems to be much advantage in using tests of primary or second-order abilities. In many cases, *g* (estimated by the score on a test such as Raven's Matrices, or from the total score on multi-aptitude batteries) gives the best prediction (Kline, 1993; 205; Thorndike, 1985). However, if it is clear from the job description that the person will be required to perform only a relatively small range of tasks (e.g. perceptual-speed tasks for a clerical post) some employers prefer to measure these abilities alone; it is

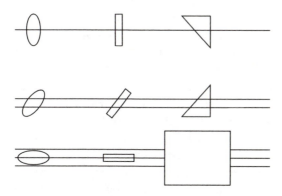

FIGURE 6.1 Typical abstract reasoning problem: what shape should fill the white box to complete the pattern?

certainly easier to justify this procedure, as the skills measured in these tests closely resemble the tasks that employees will perform.

There are also plenty of specialist tests designed for particular applications (e.g. the selection of clerks or computer programmers). Whilst many of these work well in practice, it is often not entirely clear whether they actually predict performance any better than would a test of general ability.

Performance tests

Tests such as the Crawford Small Parts Dexterity Test (Crawford and Crawford, 1956) measure manual dexterity – the person's ability to perform fiddly tasks quickly and accurately using tools such as tweezers and a screwdriver. There are also tests involving adjustable spanners, screwdrivers and nuts and bolts for would-be mechanics (Bennett, 1965), though the distinction between physical and intellectual performance soon begins to seem blurred when such tests are considered.

There are two main advantages in using standardised tests (whether individual, group or performance) rather than 'home-made' ones. The first is that users have access to tables ('norms') showing how often each score on the test is obtained in various groups of people. These may show that only one out of every hundred 16-year-old English boys gets a score above 38 on a particular test. So it is possible to tell at a glance how each individual who applies for a job compares with the norm. One might notice (for example) that *none* of the applicants for a particular post performs much above the national average on these tests, which might perhaps suggest that the post should be readvertised elsewhere so as to attract better-suited applicants. The second advantage is that these tests have (or should have!) clear evidence that they can predict performance in a variety of settings. For example, if you wanted to select a salesperson and found evidence that other firms had discovered a clear link between performance on a particular test and sales ability, one would have a good rationale for choosing to use the same test. If one developed a test oneself, there is no guarantee that it would be any good.

Work-samples

These measures are currently popular – perhaps because their clear relationship to the skills required in a particular post makes it easy for employers to defend the use of psychological tests. The logic is very simple. Following some sort of task analysis, a typical 'in tray' is concocted by a personnel manager or psychologist, containing the sorts of problems that the person will need to deal with in post. For example, all applicants for a customer relations post might be given the same few letters of complaint to follow up; their performance would then be assessed by managers. These measures are not without their problems, however – not least that of prior experience with this sort of work, which might lead to the overestimation of some applicants' potential. And what happens when the post-holder is promoted, and may need a whole set of different skills? Logically one would have to go through the same process again. Finally, as they tend to be developed for a particular organisation, these tests are not always 'validated': employers may not have hard evidence that performance on these measures is in any way linked to the candidates' future potential. Another problem is the lack of norms for such tasks. All one can do is rank-order the applicants in terms of their performance: it is impossible to tell whether all (or none) of the applicants would be likely to perform well in post.

However, it must be stressed that it is not always sensible to use ability tests as part of selection batteries. It may be that some of the skills required cannot be measured quickly and accurately by group-administered pencil-and-paper tests; dexterity and hand–eye co-ordination tends to require specialised equipment and individual testing. If the consequences of choosing the wrong individual are not too dire, then it may be cheaper to forgo any form of psychological assessment other than brief group-administered ability tests. However, if an organisation is strongly committed to identifying the very best candidates available (such as government bodies) or needs to identify individuals who will undergo fiercely expensive training programmes (such as military pilots), even very costly selection procedures can be justified.

Some empirical results

How well can scores on ability tests really predict performance? The literature here is both vast and specialised. Since about 1914 (the start of the First World War) occupational psychologists have been using a range of ability tests (of varying quality) to select individuals drawn from a still greater range of populations for an enormous variety of posts. Many of them will have calculated correlations between applicants' scores on the tests and their ultimate performance within the organisation. If this correlation is near-zero, then ability tests simply cannot predict who will succeed and who will fail within the organisation.

Trying to represent the success of all types of occupational ability testing with a single number is not particularly helpful, given that poor tests (such as those whose scores contain a lot of measurement error, 'low reliability' being the technical term), groups of applicants where there are few individual differences in ability (perhaps as a result of inviting only well-qualified applicants to sit the tests) and poor criteria of job performance (such as supervisors' ratings, where instead of using a scale in the same way, different supervisors look for different things and/or expect different standards of performance) can all undermine the size of the relationship between test-score and performance. All we can do is examine a few studies to see whether well-constructed tests really can be useful in selecting individuals for posts in industry, commerce and government.

Fortunately, there are some good reviews and analyses of the literature available. Ghiselli (1966) is a classic; more recent work (Gottfredson, 1986; Hunter, 1986; Hunter and Hunter, 1984; Kanfer *et al.*, 1995; Thorndike, 1985) generally shares the optimistic view expressed there. Cronbach (1994: 375–379) gives a case study of selecting computer programmers – where traditional variables such as college grade, age and education simply could not predict who would succeed and who would fail as trainee programmers. However, when the Computer Programmer Aptitude Battery (CPAB: Palermo, 1964) was administered to these applicants, individual tests within the CPAB were found to correlate 0.4–0.7 with performance, suggesting that the battery as a whole must have a correlation of at least 0.7. The CPAB was constructed to measure skills such as constructing and interpreting flowcharts, verbal ability (synonyms), quickly estimating solutions to numerical problems (e.g. 1,571 divided by 83 is roughly . . .), devising 'commonsense' solutions to problems and expressing data symbolically as formulae. Though the CPAB was designed to tap skills relevant to programming, most of them closely resemble scales of conventional ability tests.

Some years ago (and in a different university from my present one) we used to find that some students who enrolled for a degree in 'Psychology and Computing' encountered enormous problems with the computing modules. So I administered the CPAB, and correlated scores on this test with the students' scores on the computing modules. The correlation was 0.6, and so this test was introduced as part of a selection process for this course. Nor are large validity coefficients limited to computer programming. Hunter (1986) reviewed work with the General Aptitude Test Battery (United States Employment Service, 1979) and concluded that the 'true' relationship between a measure of general ability derived from this test and occupational performance was in the order of 0.5, though some argue that the figures point to a slightly lower value (e.g. 0.4: Hunt, 1995b).

No one asserts that general ability is the *only* variable that affects performance; motivation also plays a large part, and job knowledge may well overtake cognitive ability as a predictor of performance after an individual has been performing a particular task for some years (Kamin, 1995). However, the studies reported here are important for two reasons. The first is applied: a carefully chosen ability test can provide a useful and inexpensive means of predicting how an applicant is likely to perform within the organisation. These studies also allow us to refute a criticism that is sometimes levelled against ability tests – namely that they only predict performance on ability tests! Looking at the tables from Hunter and Hunter (1984), for example, one can see that ability tests can predict how well groups as diverse as salespersons, managers, production-line workers and drivers perform. There is also the possibility that scores on IQ tests work merely because they happen to be contaminated by other variables that happen to predict performance (Howe 1997: 98). However, as the correlation between IQ and social class (a favourite alternative explanation) is only 0.33 (White, 1982) it is difficult to see how this can cause correlations of 0.6 to emerge.

Kanfer *et al.* (1995) suggest that

> Companies have unarguably saved billions of dollars by using ability tests to assure a merit-based selection process. . . . Overall, tests of intellectual abilities are the single most predictive element in employee selection. . . and certainly more valid than the use of personal interviews. . . in predicting training and on-the-job success.
>
> (Kanfer *et al.*, 1995: 597)

Thus, there is good reason to regard occupational selection testing as one of the most useful practical achievements of psychology.

The Bell Curve

Herrnstein and Murray's (1994) book *The Bell Curve* is subtitled 'Intelligence and class structure in American life'. Its first section argues that during the course of the twentieth century the American college system became a 'meritocracy'; it was cognitive ability (rather than family or school connections, or social class) that came to influence whether a school-leaver would attend one of the more prestigious universities. Evidence for this came from scores on the Scholastic Aptitude Test (SAT) – a test used to select college students. During the 1920s and 1930s, the average SAT scores showed that the most prestigious universities were not educating the most able students.[1]

However, by the 1960s the 'ivy league' universities were attracting the most intellectually able students, who then went on

---

[1] The SAT scores are normed each year. Thus, the data should not be confounded by the 'Flynn effect', the inexorable but poorly understood increase in general mental ability from year to year.

to occupy elite posts in the professions, government and industry. Compared with the 1920s, they argue, there has been a 'cognitive partitioning', with intellectual ability (rather than wealth or background) largely determining who will rise to the top in American society, and a broadening gap between the wages paid to high-IQ and low-IQ individuals.

People tend to choose partners of similar intellectual ability ('assortive mating') and Jensen (1977) estimates the correlation between partners' levels of general ability to be approximately 0.45. As we have seen in Chapter 4, much of the evidence suggests that general ability does have some genetic component. Taken together, these two ideas imply that in a society where education is readily available and intelligence is highly valued, individuals are likely to float to a level in society that is determined by their level of general ability. Then, thanks to genetics, their descendants are more likely than not to stay there. Gould (1996: 368) reminds us that for this trend to increase and endure it is necessary to assume the validity of the concept of general ability, its genetic basis and its resistance to change – issues with which I at least have rather few problems.

The second section of *The Bell Curve* is highly relevant to the present chapter. It examines some social correlates of general ability in white Americans: for example, whether criminals (those who are caught, at any rate), lone parents, unemployed people and those in receipt of welfare benefits tend to have lower-than-average levels of general ability. More controversially Herrnstein and Murray (1994) perform analyses to determine whether *g* or social class is the better predictor of these variables: they try to determine whether their level of *g* or their social class can best predict what will happen to children. Some of these studies will be discussed below.

The third section of *The Bell Curve* examines racial differences in general ability. It is well known that in the United States the Black and Latino communities perform less well than the white majority (or other minority groups, such as the Chinese). The average level of general ability for Black Americans is about a standard deviation lower than for whites. Quite why this should be is still a matter of hot debate. There are three possibilities.

(a) The difference may be due to culturally biased tests, lower motivation to achieve and other nutritional, social, cultural and economic variables that mean that the tests are unfair to members of the Black community – that is, that their test scores underestimate their true level of ability.

(b) The second view is that the difference is genuine; that there is a full standard-deviation difference in the levels of g in the two groups.

(c) Third, there is a compromise view – that the tests are to some extent unfair, but that such factors cannot fully explain the disparity. That is, there may still be a difference in mean general ability scores between the groups, but this will be less than a standard deviation.

I do not propose entering the debate about group differences in general ability – partly because it is not relevant to this chapter, partly because I dislike the idea of considering groups of people rather than individuals, and partly because it is a short step to assuming that *all* members of one group are superior to *any* member of another (as in the 1930s), and because it is offensive to use crude generalisations such as this. Brody (1992: ch 10) gives what seems to be an eminently fair commentary on these issues for those who wish to follow it up.

The Bell Curve has received many hostile reviews from those who see it as a right-wing attempt to justify racist attitudes through hijacking a psychological model. The book *The Bell Curve Debate* (Jacoby and Glauberman, 1995) contains a number of counter-arguments from a variety of perspectives (and of variable quality). *Intelligence, Genes & Success* (Devlin *et al.*, 1997) contains some first-rate chapters; several Internet sites and discussion groups consider the book from more or less informed viewpoints. However, it is good science to ensure that one actually reads the book rather than just reading reviews of it.

The second section of *The Bell Curve* (which scrutinises the link between ability and real-world performance) does, in any case, give plenty of food for thought. The remainder of this chapter will consider some of the analyses of white Americans discussed in that section, as these may shed some light on the social consequences of having high g without so many political overtones. The main thesis of this section of *The Bell Curve* is that g helps individuals to function well in society, and so low levels of g will be associated with poverty, crime, divorce and a lack of typical middle-class values.

Methodological issues

Little attention is paid to 'goodness of fit'

Herrnstein and Murray's raw data came from the National Longitudinal Survey of Youth (NLSY), a study which has since 1979 traced the progress of children after leaving school (see the web site at http://www.bls.gov/nlshome.htm). The data-set is valuable as it is based on a large (12,000+ before removing those of Black and Latino origin) representative sample of Americans who were aged 14–22 at the start of testing. However, some of the analyses in *The Bell Curve* are based on much smaller sub-samples than this; fewer than 1,000 in some cases. It contains data on the childhood environment, parental socio-economic status, educational and employment history, details of family formation plus scores on the 'Armed Forces Qualification Test' (AFQT) – a measure of general ability that is discussed quite extensively in Appendix 3 of Herrnstein and Murray (1994). Few reviewers of the book have commented adversely on the quality of the test used, whatever their other objections.

The analyses use well-known statistical techniques called logistic regression and multiple regression in an attempt to discover how well their social background (parents' socio-economic status, SES, which is a mixture of their education, occupation and income) and/or cognitive ability can predict various criterion behaviours, such as number of children, or imprisonment. Multiple regression is used when the thing being predicted (e.g. annual income) is a continuous number; logistic regression is used when it is a two-valued number (yes/no).

Herrnstein and Murray plot the relationships between SES, AFQT-scores and social phenomena as graphs – for example, showing how the probability of some social phenomenon (such as being a low-birth-weight baby) varies as a function of the mother's SES or general ability. But the raw data points are not shown. All that *is* shown is a 'line of best fit' placed through these points. To see why this is dangerous, consider Figure 6.2. Without seeing the raw data points (the circles or crosses in Figure 6.2 it is impossible to tell whether the line provides a good fit to the data points (as with the crosses) or a very poor approximation (as with the circles). A statistic called R^2 shows how good the prediction is when performing multiple regression; it lies between 0 and 1. If R^2 is 0.33, this implies that 33 per cent of the variation in the thing being assessed (annual income, or whatever) can be 'explained' by the other variables (e.g. social class, score on the ability test), and that $1-0.33 = 0.67$ of the variation is due to other things. Logistic regression does not produce an R^2 statistic, but some approximations have been developed which

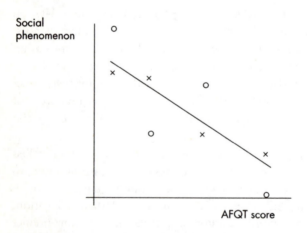

FIGURE 6.2   Diagram showing how the same regression line may show either a good fit to the data (crosses) or rather poor fit (circles)

are shown in Herrnstein and Murray's book. The key thing to remember is that a large R^2 means that the data fit the model well; a small value implies prediction that is no better than chance.[2] To tell which models fit the data and which manifestly do not, it is necessary to flick to Appendix 4 of *The Bell Curve* and examine the values of R^2 for each model.

The graphs showing social performance as a function of g or SES may not be linear

Hunt (1995a) makes the eminently sensible point that the psychometrician's approach (looking for a simple, linear relationship between ability/SES and social outcomes) may be flawed. Instead of there being a gradual link between ability and social factors, he suggests that 'intelligence scores in the bottom 15 per cent almost always indicate that a person has a substantial risk of encountering problems in our society'. Above this level there may be no discernible relationship between ability and performance in society, which will result in the linear model not fitting very well (hence the low R-squared values).

Other possible difficulties

Other difficulties include the fairly high correlation between SES and AFQT scores (0.55 according to Hunt, 1995a) which may cause a problem called 'collinearity', probable small numbers of cases in some of the analyses (for example, the book does not tell us how *many* high-SES individuals were interviewed in jail) and the need to assume that SES was estimated reliably, and with a good range of scores. However, Hunt mentions that

---

[2] Herrnstein and Murray do report the results of tests showing whether the slopes of the curves for AFQT and SES are significantly different from zero. A well-known problem of regression is that these tests are invariably significant for large sample sizes, and the AFQT sample is based on several thousand individuals. A statistic that does not rely on sample size (such as R^2) gives a much better view of what is going on.

there have been a number of privately-circulated alternative analyses of the NLSY data. All the ones that I have seen show that, although you might change the exact numbers reported by Herrnstein and Murray a bit, intelligence is a substantial predictor of indicators of social problems.

(Hunt, 1995a: 1)

Results from The Bell Curve

Table 6.1 summarises the main results from the second section of Herrnstein and Murray (1994). These analyses are based on the AFQT results of various groups, and are reported by Herrnstein and Murray on the pages shown in column 1. For clarity I have not gone into great detail about how the samples were selected. All analyses controlled for differences in age statistically. In addition, other necessary criteria were included: for example, when analysing the number of people who had ever married by age 30, only those who were aged 30 or more were considered. This is why the sample sizes (shown in column 3) vary from analysis to analysis.

Column 4 shows how well each model fitted the data. A large value here implies that the analysis really allows one to make rather accurate predictions about an individual's behaviour given a knowledge of their age, parents' SES and AQFT-scores (plus other variables shown in column 3). A value of zero implies that the model is useless for making predictions. Finally, the figures in columns 5 and 6 show the relative importance of the AFQT and SES scores for predicting the behaviour. They are not correlations. But (like correlations) the sign of these numbers shows the direction of the relationship.

It can be seen from these analyses that the models reported by Herrnstein and Murray are rather good at predicting who will drop out of high school, gain a college degree or (for women) be on welfare benefit within a year of the birth of their first child. They have some success in forecasting who will fall below the poverty line, be interviewed in jail, adopt middle-class values, or

TABLE 6.1 Relative importance of Armed Forces Qualification Test (AFQT) and parents' socio-economic status (SES) as predictors of the probability of various life events

Page	Probability of (controlling for age, in each case)	R^2	N of cases	AFQT beta	SES beta
134/596	Being below the poverty line	0.10	3367	−0.83	−0.33
149/597	Dropping out of high school	0.34	3572	−1.72	−0.64
152/598	Gaining a bachelor's degree	0.37	3821	1.81	1.04
159/599	Out of work for a month or more	0.02	1686	−0.36	0.22
172/601	Ever being married by age 30 for those with only high-school education	0.03	605	0.51	−0.11
175/601	Divorce in first five years of marriage	0.02	2031	−0.36	0.22
183/604	Illegitimate first birth (women)	0.08	604	−0.65	−0.30
195/607	Women on welfare after birth of first child, controlling for pre-birth poverty and marital status	0.31	839	−0.58	−0.06
215/610	Women having a low-birth-weight infant controlling for pre-birth poverty	0.03	1864	−0.46	0.03
249/621	Male ever interviewed in jail	0.10	1945	−0.90	−0.16
265	Middle-class values	0.08	3029	0.63	0.24

Source: Herrnstein and Murray (1994), pages as shown in column 1

(for women) have their first child outside marriage. They are not very good at predicting any of the other phenomena shown in the table, and discussed in some detail in the main text of the book.

Surprisingly, the main body of the text never recognises that some of the models provide woefully poor fit to the data. One of the weakest relationships shown in Table 6.1 is that between scores on the measure of general ability (AFQT), SES and the probability of being out of the labour force for a month or more. Yet these data are interpreted as if they fitted the model near-perfectly. For example,

> It is not hard to imagine why high intelligence helps keep a man at work ... competence in the workplace is related to intelligence, and competent people more than incompetent people are likely to find the workplace a congenial and rewarding place. Hence, other things equal, they are more likely than incompetent people to be in the labor force.
>
> Herrnstein and Murray, (1994: 159–160)

The actual degree of prediction is little better than chance.

In each case the scores on the measure of general ability (AFQT) seems to be better than parental SES in predicting the criterion behaviours; it seems that high levels of general ability may well be a useful predictor of some aspects of the way in which people behave in society – albeit rather fewer than those claimed by Herrnstein and Murray. All of this begs a rather interesting question. If Herrnstein and Murray's thesis about social stratification is correct, one would expect few (if any) high-IQ parents in the very bottom social strata, or low-IQ parents at the top of the SES range. If general ability is substantially genetic in origin – and here Herrnstein and Murray (1994: 108) believe in a value of about 0.6 – how many high-IQ/low-parental-SES or low-IQ/high-parental-SES teenagers were in the sample? One would suspect that rather few individuals would fall into these cells, which may raise problems for the analyses.

Herrnstein and Murray's book has generated an enormous amount of debate, not all of it well informed. It certainly does seem that there are a few links between general ability and performance in American culture. However, some of the strongest of these are those related to educational outcome (e.g. gaining a college degree). It would be truly amazing if general ability were *not* related to such academic outcomes! And the problem with some of the other analyses is that there are likely to be a large number of confounding variables, all of which cannot be examined given the sample sizes available to Herrnstein and Murray. For example, given that a substantial proportion of the most intellectually able students spend some years at college, it seems probable that fewer of them will choose to interrupt their studies in order to have a baby (inside or outside marriage) than those who are working or living on benefit. So it is perhaps unsurprising that fewer high-IQ women have had a baby outside marriage during the period of the study. So even if some aspects of their work does suggest a modest link between general ability and various life events, it is not at all clear that the link is causal. When the data shown in the back of *The Bell Curve* are scrutinised, there is not *that* much evidence for the apocalyptic *g*-based model of social stratification outlined in the first section of that book.

Summary

This chapter considered whether tests of ability are able to predict real-life behaviour, or whether they are merely of interest to academic psychologists. The first section considered some various types of ability tests, and pointed to the inadvisability of working out a sort of 'average prediction power' of all sorts of tests used to predict a huge range of behaviours within an enormous range of samples. Instead we referred interested readers to the detailed literature, whilst noting that the predictive power of ability tests can under some circumstances be very substantial. Indeed, it is difficult to think of any job or occupation where low *g* is associated with high performance.

The second half of the chapter introduced a controversial book, Herrnstein and Murray's (1994) *The Bell Curve*, which has become notorious because one section focuses on racial differences in general ability. We focused on the second section of this book, which analysed whether general ability or social class is the better predictor of a range of social phenomena, ranging from school/college performance through unemployment to having a low birth-weight baby. However, we suggested that there is a serious problem with these analyses that has not been recognised in the literature. Herrnstein and Murray failed to consider how well each of the models fits the data. If one tried to predict whether or not a person would (for example) be out of work for a month or more on the basis of social class and general ability (as advocated by Herrnstein and Murray) the prediction would be very little better than would be obtained by guessing. Indeed, of the eleven variables considered here, only three can be adequately predicted from social class and general ability: dropping out of high school, gaining a bachelor's degree, and being on welfare after the birth of a first child. Rather than showing that low *g* is the source of all society's ills, Herrnstein and Murray's own analyses suggested rather modest or non-existent relationships between general ability, social class, and people's behaviour in society.

Further reading

Gottfredson, L. (1997) 'Why *g* matters: the complexity of everyday life', *Intelligence* 24: 79–132. Demonstrates that and explains why *g* is important in everyday life.

Herrnstein, R.J. and Murray, C. (1994) *The Bell Curve: Intelligence and Class Structure in American Life*, New York: The Free Press. Chapters 5–12 consider how *g* and social class explain a number of social phenomena outlined in Table 6.1.

Kline, P. (1991) *Intelligence: The Psychometric View;* London: Routledge. Chapter Five discusses some links between intelligence and educational/occupational success.

Thorndike, R.L. (1985) 'The central role of general ability in prediction', *Multivariate Behavioral Research* 20: 241–254. Evidence for the predictive utility of *g*.

Chapter 7

Overview

The science and technology of human abilities

The purpose of this chapter is to draw out the main themes from the rest of this book, mention (and offer references to) any contentious issues and stress the implications of the research discussed above for both the theory of mental abilities and its practical application – such as in educational, occupational and clinical psychology. It is useful to think in terms of the science and technology of individual differences. Science is the attempt to understand (and therefore to be able to predict) complex events; technology the application of scientific knowledge and principles to real-life problems. Questions addressed by science include the behaviour of various chemicals, the motion of objects, the behaviour of economies, and weather systems. The related technologies would include the development and large-scale production of useful chemicals (e.g. glues, paints), rocket systems for launching satellites, the development of economic strategies to avoid cycles of unsustainable economic growth and recession, and prediction of earthquakes. In the psychology of abilities, the technology involves developing tests to assess the various abilities, and using these to solve real-life problems.

Science operates by trying to develop simple models that fit the observed data reasonably well, and then modifying these whenever necessary. For example, Newton's laws of motion were quite adequate when understanding how objects (such as snooker balls) behave when they hit each other, but when scientists came to study the behaviour of much smaller particles, Newton's laws failed to predict what actually happened. So a more complex model was developed that explained behaviour of both large and small objects (quantum-mechanics and the theory of relativity).

The first step in any scientific enterprise involves conceptualising the field of study: deciding which properties are important when studying moving bodies, which chemical elements show similar properties to others, and which variables influence economies and the weather. Then it is necessary to explain precisely why these laws work, in terms of still simpler processes: this will generally involve some sort of mathematical model. Why do chemical elements combine in certain proportions (e.g. one part magnesium, one part, sodium and four parts oxygen) to form compounds (magnesium sulphate), but not in some other proportions? Why does inflation start? What causes hurricanes?

The structure of abilities

Psychology, too, needs to determine the most appropriate way of conceptualising a complex field: it needs something akin to the chemist's periodic table or the biologist's system for classifying animals into families, orders, etc. in order to highlight regularities within a complex mass of data. Only then is it possible to explore the really interesting questions of what *causes* individual differences in these abilities to come about

When studying individual differences in intelligence and abilities, the main problem is that there is an infinite number of different tasks that require thought for their successful completion. So surely it is necessary to consider many thousands of different abilities when developing a model? Fortunately, the results from factor-analytic studies (described in Chapter 2) show that this is incorrect, as there is rather a lot of overlap (correlation) between people's scores on different tasks. Because of this, it is possible to conceptualise the main cognitive abilities in terms of twenty or so 'primary mental abilities'. This list cannot be exhaustive (esoteric abilities such as those involved in detecting whether a surface is curved or flat through rubbing it with the fingers will not be included), but there is reason to believe that these twenty primary mental abilities describe much of our day-to-day cognitive activity.

The method of factor analysis also shows that these twenty primary mental abilities are themselves correlated, and so that the best way to conceptualise abilities is via a hierarchical model. Some of the primary abilities tend to rise and fall together from person to person. Thus they form five or so distinct (but correlated) 'second-order abilities' – visualisation, retrieval, fluid and crystallised ability and cognitive speed. And all of *these* abilities form a 'third-order' factor of general ability.

This structure is a matter of empirical fact: there is not much theory associated with it. The methods used to identify 'similar' abilities are, in fact, remarkably similar to those used by biologists to identify 'similar' species, when building taxonomic systems (e.g. Sokal and Sneath, 1963). It is tempting to try to develop a model of abilities by looking at the types of tasks involved. Ignoring factor analysis we could group all tasks that involve written language together, bundle all tasks involving numbers into a second group, and so on. Unfortunately, such models are unlikely to describe how people actually perform in practice, and so will be of little use. We saw in Chapter 2 that verbal ability (tasks such as vocabulary, comprehension of knowledge of proverbs, grammar) form a primary ability factor. But *other* tasks that also involve language (such as those asking people to think of creative uses for objects, to think of words quickly) form quite *different* factors. So whilst one might *think* that a common 'language skill' must affect performance on all tests involving language, the evidence from the factor analytic studies shows that this is wrong. The beauty of factor analysis is that it identifies groups of tasks that really are similar – not those which someone thinks *ought* to be similar.

Simply knowing the structure of abilities is useful for three main reasons.

- First, it guides practitioners (clinical psychologists, occupational psychologists, educational psychologists) who want to assess an individual's mental abilities – perhaps to determine whether someone who has suffered a stroke is intellectually impaired, to see if a child has any particular strengths or weaknesses, or to select the best applicant for a job. It is possible to construct psychological tests only if knows the

structure of ability as it is an important principle of psychometrics that each scale of a test should measure a single
factor, and one cannot tell this other than by knowing the
structure of abilities. The finding that there is a factor of
general ability (g) at the top of the hierarchy indicates that
one way of measuring intellectual potential would be to give
a person a test of general ability, involving abstract
reasoning. Or moving down the hierarchy one could measure
the second-order abilities: crystallised ability (which will
reflect knowledge and quality of schooling), fluid ability
(similar to g), retrieval and spatial ability. If one wants a
still more detailed picture, one could assess the twenty or
so primary abilities.

- Second, it suggests how researchers should try to develop
  process models. For example, the presence of a 'verbal
  ability' primary factor suggests that there are substantial
  individual differences in various language-related skills.
  What causes these to emerge? It would be possible to
  examine the relative importance of amount and quality of
  schooling, speed of certain language-related cognitive
  processes (e.g. retrieving the meaning of a word from
  memory), genetics, amount of reading experience, etc. on
  language ability. This sort of work can be enormously
  important for informing and shaping educational policy, as
  it can suggest interventions that may be able to enhance the
  performance of the next generation of children.

- Third, the structural model also has implications for other
  branches of psychology. The empirical finding that there are
  several different memory factors, for example, suggests that
  rather different processes are involved when storing and
  recalling meaningless material (pairs of nonsense-words such
  as 'sab-gop', semantically related material (e.g. 'cringing-
  elephant') and lists of numbers to be retained for just a few
  seconds (as in a telephone number). It just so happens that
  cognitive psychology had already reached much the same
  conclusion from a rather different starting-point, but if it
  had not, factor analysis would have been useful in directing

cognitive research. The cognitive processes involved in primary abilities such as original uses for objects, fluency of ideas and word fluency do not seem to be particularly well understood in terms of cognitive psychology: perhaps this may be a useful area to research.

Alternatives to factor analysis

Sternberg's triarchic theory

Chapter 3 included three other views of the nature and structure of abilities, in order to show some of the more recent developments and debates about this most fundamental issue. Sternberg's triarchic theory is enormously complex, and takes a much broader definition of 'ability' than that assumed in Chapter 2: indeed, it is difficult to draw much of a distinction between ability, motivation and personality within Sternberg's theory.

One of its great strengths of the componential sub-theory is that it introduces 'metacomponents' – planning how to conceptualise and solve problems, devising strategies and so on – as well as performance components. The types of tasks used to determine the structure of abilities through factor analysis are much simpler, and may offer little or no scope for planning or devising efficient strategies.

Sternberg's view of intelligence as being effective interaction between an individual and their environment (the contextual sub-theory) is intuitively appealing, yet difficult to test. After all, the cognitive processes for appraising and interpreting an environment are themselves likely to be complex, and influenced by factors other than abilities. We have all met individuals who are perpetually depressed, unhappy and unlikely to make an effective adaptation to any environment, or view *any* alternative environment as offering more opportunities. Does this mean that they are not intelligent? And the appraisal of an 'environment' is necessarily subjective: it is difficult to imagine that many people will be objective when evaluating their family home, the prospect of a 9 a.m. lecture on Monday in winter, or a loved-one's circle of friends. Mood, motivation and personality are likely to complicate the appraisals, and thus (indirectly) the decision of how to adapt.

The experiential sub-theory seems to be much more useful: it suggests that certain processes (such as selective encoding of information, automaticity) are important in problem-solving where the task and/or situation is novel.

Overall, the model has two main problems.

- It makes a rather radical redefinition of 'intelligence' which involves the social context and social significance of behaviour, previous experience, and the sorts of high-level planning skills that may well be important in everyday life but which have been refined out of most conventional ability tests. The 'smart' thing to do might even be to deliberately achieve a poor grade on an ability test, if avoiding parental pressure or keeping with one's peer group are highly valued goals.

- It views 'intelligence' as being the product of a complex series of processes: basic cognitive operations (thinking, planning), the role of prior experience, and environmental pressures and constraints. The more complex a model, the harder it is to test its correctness (witness Freud's psychoanalytic model of personality), which is why science generally starts with a very simple model and expands it piecemeal in ways that continually improve the accuracy of its predictions.

It has been argued (e.g. Kline, 1991) that some of its terms are non-contingent concepts: they must *necessarily* exist, making some aspects of the theory incapable of being falsified. This makes the theory unscientific, according to some views of the philosophy of science. For example, it is impossible to start solving a problem without planning how to do so, thus there are *bound* to be some planning components. Encoding is a process that basically involves assimilating (reading and understanding the meaning of) the raw data of the problem one is trying to solve. How can one tackle a problem without performing some encoding? However, this objection to Sternberg's work seems to miss the point: if there are stable individual differences in the amount of time taken to execute such processes, this process is potentially capable of predicting individual differences in the solution time of complex tasks. The important thing is to show that the amount of time taken to perform such cognitive activities is stable within an individual over time, and across problems.

The triarchic model is important in that it tries to broaden the whole scope of research into intelligence: it reminds academic psychologists that there may be more to 'intelligence' than mere abstract reasoning. The theory sprang from Sternberg's attempts to model abilities in terms of the durations and sequencing of a few cognitive processes. As well as this type of research, it has spawned much interest in social intelligence (e.g. picking up cues from body-language), skills such as prioritising demands on one's time that one picks up 'on the job' rather than through instruction or training, and the role of novelty of task and situation on problem-solving.

Jensen (1998: 132) observes that there is little in Sternberg's theory that is antithetical to g (or any of the other ability factors discussed in Chapter 2): *something* causes individual differences in the performance components and metacomponents, and this may well be g, the primary mental abilities or the second-order abilities discussed in Chapter 2. The experiential and contextual aspects of Sternberg's theories may 'reflect achievement variables that reflect how different individuals invest in activities as affected by their particular opportunities, interests, personality traits, and motivation' (Jensen, 1998) Ultimately the important issue is whether one chooses to define intelligence in much the same way as Spearman, Thurstone and Cattell (that is, as cognitive ability), or to broaden the definition to include (rather than control for) individual differences in personality, experience and motivation on cognitive performance.

As yet Sternberg's work has had little impact on the technology of ability testing, and conventional ability tests have not been thrown over in favour of measures of environmental adaptation, motivation, planning or automatisation. This may well be for pragmatic reasons: the last thing that practising psychologists need is tests that take ever longer to administer.

Gardner's theory of multiple intelligences

We argued in Chapter 3 that there is really rather little incompatibility between Gardner's model of abilities and the factor-analytic model previously discussed. Though stemming from rather different sources (a review of the literature in order to determine which groups of abilities change as a result of brain damage, maturation, etc. versus empirical studies of how people perform when faced with different types of problems) several of Gardner's 'intelligences' seem to correspond to the main abilities discovered through factor analysis. Those that do not (such as social intelligence) simply fall outside the conventional, cognitive, definition of intelligence used by the factor theorists. The other problem with Gardner's theory is that it is not quantitative: there are no tests available for measuring the different intelligences, which makes it difficult to test whether they are the same as conventional ability factors, whether they add to the efficacy of g when predicting behaviour, or even whether they are correlated together.

This last point is crucial. Much of the appeal of Gardner's model has been in education, where teachers are understandably keen to adopt a model which allows them to take a positive view of children's abilities and potentials. So what if Mary does not burst with linguistic intelligence: with six other 'intelligences' to choose from, there is likely to be at least one at which she will excel. For example, her social intelligence may be excellent, which may suit her wonderfully for a career in sales or marketing. Drawing this inference *assumes* that Gardner's 'intelligences' are uncorrelated, even though we know from empirical data (the hierarchical model of abilities) that ability factors are almost invariably correlated. This means that if children perform well below average in one area, they are also less likely to excel in other areas. If Gardner's 'intelligences' were shown to be correlated, the theory would lose much of its appeal for teachers.

Howe's criticisms

Howe suggests that factor analysis is unable to reveal the structure of abilities, and that in any case it would be quite wrong to assume that an ability factor is anything more than a convenient description of the way in which people behave: it does not imply that anything 'inside them' *causes* the factor to emerge. Claims about the genetic basis of intelligence are unwarranted (although only separated identical twins are considered), learning and experience may account for the correlations between measures such as inspection time and *g*, and 'generally speaking, IQ scores do not generate predictions [of behaviour] that are better than random guesses' (Howe, 1997: 96). Howe's view is that 'factor analysis does not actually "find" any pattern' when applied to test scores, as 'there may be a number of alternative patterns to be discerned, and factor analysis does not identify any one pattern that is uniquely present in the data' (1997: 28). In short, he maintains that the widespread belief that general intelligence (or any other form of ability) exists inside us, is biological in nature, is genetically transmitted, is difficult or impossible to change and is useful in predicting behaviour simply fails to stand up to scrutiny. Several of these issues have been addressed in the text: it is necessary here to draw out the implications of these findings.

The main thrust of this work seems to be that whilst ability factors may give one (of many possible) descriptions of abilities, there is little point in trying to understand individual differences in such performance in terms of 'internal' factors such as genetic makeup or the psychophysiology of the nervous system. Unfortunately, Howe does not offer hard data to support his assertion that the model of abilities is arbitrary. The idea that factor analysis cannot lead to replicable solutions is a somewhat technical one, which was generally reckoned to have been resolved by Thurstone's (1947) concept of 'simple structure'; my reading of the literature is that there has been rather substantial replication of a hierarchical model of ability (e.g. Carroll, 1993; Gustafsson, 1981; Hakstian and Cattell, 1978) with Gardner's work also offering some support for the main ability factors. Carroll (1997b) gives an excellent summary of the literature.

When it comes to examining the correlations between reaction times, inspection times, EEG measures and abilities, the basic question is how large a (statistically significant) correlation has to be before it indicates a really substantive relationship. Howe (1997: 31) is not convinced that correlations in the order of 0.4 indicate a substantial relationship; others take a different view. It is further suggested that scores on ability test parental social class, educational opportunities, interests, etc. (Howe, 1997: 98). Thus, if ability tests are substantially correlated with performance (which he conceded is sometimes the case) such correlations may arise because the test scores reflect these all-important characteristics. Yet *The Bell Curve* consistently suggests that parental social class does *not* underlie the correlations between *g* and life events.

As far as the applications of Howe's objections are concerned, one could argue for a pragmatic view. If an employer needs to appoint someone with good numerical skills, a test of numerical ability will identify who should be employed. It matters not a jot whether these skills stem from genes, an interest in mathematics, a good teacher or parental encouragement. All that the employer wants is someone who can manipulate numbers. Thus, I am not sure that Howe's comments will have much impact on the ways in which tests are actually used.

Process models

Notwithstanding Howe's reservations about scientific reductionism, the consistent discovery of certain ability factors by researchers using different sets of cognitive tasks, different samples of participants and different forms of factor analysis has driven some workers to try to understand why such factors come about: that is, why certain skills tend to vary together between individuals. General ability (*g*) in particular has been studied extensively, and quite a lot is now known about its underpinnings.

It is difficult for even the most dogged environmentalist to claim that general ability is unrelated to an individual's genetic makeup. Although various genetically informative research designs (e.g family studies, twin studies, adoption studies) each have their problems, some simple designs ignore the possibly of interactions between genes and so will tend to overestimate the importance of genetic influences, and the memory of the 'Burt affair' lingers on, the results of hundreds of studies virtually all point in the same direction. General ability has a substantial genetic component, and we are starting to identify the individual genes that are involved in intelligent behaviour. As genes control the structure and function of the nervous system, it thus seems reasonable to view general ability as a biological process as well as something that is environmentally determined.

It should of course be remembered that even though a variable has a genetic basis, this does not mean that a particular child's future is mapped out at conception: there is still plenty of scope for the environment to influence intellectual performance. If they receive a lucky throw of the genetic dice, children who are brought up in very difficult, unsupportive environments may still shine intellectually – which seems to be a much more encouraging prospect than having one's future mapped out by one's parents' social status.

The theoretical implications of this work are considerable. Finding that simple perceptual variables (e.g. inspection time) or physiological measures (e.g. the EEG) measured in the laboratory correlate appreciably with scores on paper-and-pencil tests of reasoning is encouraged, but needs to be included in a theoretical model of neural functioning. Eysenck and Jensen's early model (Eysenck, 1967; Jensen and Munroe, 1974) (which suggested that general ability is a result of speed or accuracy of neural transmission) has not been well supported by direct studies of neural conduction velocity, and it is a totally global model that does not attempt to consider the localisation of cognitive functioning within the brain, hemispheric specialisation or the distinction between input and output processes. Unfortunately, neuroscientists are frequently more interested in the *nature* of processing at various brain sites than in individual differences in cognitive performance (overlooking Cronbach's plea for integration outlined in Chapter 1), whilst those working with neural nets also fail to consider why certain individuals take longer to process information than do others. Rather little seems to have changed since Posner *et al.* (1988) observed that:

> most neuroscience network theories of higher processes provide little information on the specific computations performed at the nodes of the network, and most cognitive network models provide little or no information on the anatomy involved.
>
> (Posner *et al.*, 1988)

Alternative models have indeed been suggested – see Barrett (1997) and Willis and Aspel (1994) for some brief reviews – but none has yet received widespread support. Thus, rather little is yet known about what is taking place at a neuronal level during problem-solving, where it takes place or the ways in which complex problems are broken down and passed to different functional systems for their solution.

Once again, the direct practical implications of this work are less obvious than their theoretical import. There was a of interest in inspection time when an early study reported a correlation of –0.9 between inspection time and scores on a standard intelligence test (Nettelbeck and Lally, 1976). Before the statistical problems of this study were appreciated, clinical psychologists speculated whether it might be possible to replace their standard hour-long individual tests of ability with a simple ten-minute perceptual task. We are a long way from that point at present.

Abilities in everyday life

Even Howe (1997) acknowledges that ability tests can show moderate-to-high relationships with life events such as job performance and educational success. We have seen examples of how selection tests may be useful in applied psychology, whilst educational and clinical psychologists find such measures useful for detecting unusual (high or low) abilities, or specific problems (e.g. a good non-verbal skills but markedly lower levels of verbal ability, perhaps suggesting dyslexia). We have also seen how *The Bell Curve* (Herrnstein and Murray, 1994) claims that general ability, g, is a potent predictor of a great many social phenomena, ranging from early pregnancy and welfare-dependency to criminal behaviour.

We have suggested that not all of these models fit the data spectacularly well. Leaving such objections aside, this work raises the spectre of a 'cognitive underclass', individuals with below-average ability who are appreciably more likely than high-ability individuals to experience low income, jail, unemployment, and who are more likely to have low-birth-weight children and not vote in elections. Remember, all these relationships hold after controlling statistically for the effects of social class: one of the key points made by Herrnstein and Murray is that parental social class is a much worse predictor of all these phenomena than is general ability.

As there do not seem to be *any* personal or social draw-backs to having a high level of general ability, it may make sense for a society to try to boost the cognitive performance of chil-dren – for example, through educational interventions, vitamin supplements, parental education, or through attempting to change attitudes to and motivation towards education. So psychological and educational research may inform political decision-making. Fortunately, however, the average general ability of children spon-taneously increases from generation to generation (the 'Flynn effect') for reasons that are poorly understood. If this trend continues (which it has done so for almost a century) and levels of general ability do determine social outcomes, then one might perhaps expect to see an improvement in society over the years.

It is not obvious whether any intervention that is applied to all children in society will change the rank-ordering of children's general ability. Do we assume that some children's cognitive performance is being held back by some adverse life event, whilst others reach their full potential? In this case it is quite possible that changing the quality of life for the disadvantaged children may change their ranking relative to others. Or do we assume that an intervention (e.g. teaching reading earlier by a new method, or providing nursery education) will boost the general ability of *all* children by a certain amount? If *this* is the case, the rank-ordering of the children will stay precisely the same. This is a crucial issue, and can really be resolved only by understanding the process underpinning general ability.

This whole area is also politically highly sensitive: the far right point to evidence suggesting that general ability is substantially heritable, and suggest that as lower-ability parents produce more children than do higher-ability parents, levels of intelligence ought to be declining over time. Though as we have seen, the opposite is true (Flynn, 1987). The extreme left reject the idea of mental testing, general ability and (particularly) its genetic basis on principle, and stress the importance of environmental interventions and developing the individuality of each child.

There is also a more sinister argument. It has been found that American Blacks score substantially lower (about half a standard deviation lower) than do American whites on ability tests, though whether this is due to environmental effects (poor housing, schools, nutrition), cultural values or genetic differences is not at all well understood. Herrnstein and Murray's data linking social phenomena to general ability were drawn from a sample of white Americans: it is possible for the political right to suggest that as general ability determines performance in society *and* Black Americans are lower in general ability than white Americans *therefore* Black Americans should remain in menial jobs, will inevitably be overrepresented in prison, etc. Herrnstein and Murray's data may be used to support racist attitudes. The assumptions that are made during this process are often ignored. For it is necessary to assume that:

- the IQ difference is genuine (rather than caused by tests that are biased against – i.e. more difficult for – members of the Black community
- the relationship between general ability is the same within the Black community as within the white (identical regression equations)

- standards of economic deprivation are similar for the two groups, or racial differences in general ability are genetic in origin
- interventions will either have no effect or will boost the ability of *all* children (not just those with specific social problems).

Those interested in pursuing such issues are advised to consult Devlin *et al.* (1997) or Jacoby and Glauberman (1995).

The debate over the social consequences of general ability has cast the spotlight on what was, until then, a fairly uncontentious branch of psychology. It has also led to a proliferation of views that sometimes seem to owe more to politics than to empirical science (e.g. the rejection of the body of evidence suggesting that general ability is to some extent influenced by our genetic makeup). It is becoming ever more obvious that in order to address the issues arising from the *Bell Curve* debate, we need to improve our understanding of the basic processes that bring about individual differences in cognitive ability, so that if indeed it is better to be born intelligent than rich (as Herrnstein and Murray, 1994 suggest) then at least we can give our children every opportunity in life.

Glossary

The first occurrence of each of these terms is highlighted in **bold** type in the main text.

alpha activity Brain electrical activity that has between eight and thirteen 'peaks' a second, and which is usually found when a person is alert.

analogies Problems such as 'cat is to kitten as dog is to . . .'

behaviour genetics The study of how genes influence behaviour.

choice reaction time A reaction time (q.v.) measured where there are several lights to be monitored and the nature of the response depends on which light is illuminated (e.g. pressing a button by the light).

circular explanation Trying to explain behaviour using a factor inferred from observing behaviour, e.g. inferring that people are anxious because they tremble, and then explaining that the trembling is caused by anxiety.

cognitive psychology The branch of psychology that tries to understand the general laws of

memory, thought, language, perception, etc. – though not individual differences in these phenomena.

common environment   Any aspects of the environment that tend to make children brought up together similar, e.g. parental attitudes, culture, number of books at home.

component   Sternberg's term for a 'thinking operation' either involved with planning ('metacomponent'), seeking information ('knowledge acquisition component') or executing ('performance component') some task.

componential analysis   An experimental design for estimating the durations of various performance components (q.v.) in Sternberg's triarchic theory.

componential sub-theory   The 'cognitive' branch of Sternberg's triarchic theory. It seeks to explain how an individual conceptualises and solves a particular task, using metacomponents and performance components.

contextual sub-theory   The part of Sternberg's triarchic theory that views intelligence as optimising the interaction between the individual and the environment.

correlation   A statistic that varies from –1 to + 1. A correlation of 0 implies that two variables (tests) are completely different: a low score on one test does not imply that a score on a second test will be lower or higher than the norm. A correlation of + 1 implies that scores on one test are exactly proportional to scores on the other. A correlation of –1 implies that scores on one test are inversely proportional to scores on the other. A correlation such as 0.5 would imply that if people have an above-average on one test, they are more likely than not to have an above-average score on the second test – but the relationship is not perfect.

EEG or electroencephalogram   Measurement of electrical activity in the brain from electrodes stuck onto the scalp.

elementary cognitive operation   Carroll's term for some basic thought process that takes a fixed amount of time to complete. e.g. recovering the meaning of a word from memory.

evoked potential recording   The pattern of electrical activity in the brain that follows some event (such as a sound or flash of light).

experiential sub-theory   The part of Sternberg's triarchic theory that seeks to understand how complex tasks come to be performed automatically.

factor analysis A statistical technique that can determine whether a group of mental tests measure one or several distinct abilities through examining the correlation between test scores.

factors Groups of tests that measure the same ability, e.g. tests of addition, subtraction and geometry may measure an 'arithmetical ability' factor.

fraternal twins Twins who share only half of those genes on which humans vary, and who are thus no more genetically similar than any other pair of siblings.

g Spearman's factor of general ability, implying that a person tended to perform at a similar level (relative to his or her peers) on *all types* of ability test.

genes Chemicals passed on from our parents that control the way cells develop, and which may thus affect abilities through their influence on the structure of the nervous system.

genetic Inherited, as opposed to socially determined.

heritability The extent to which a particular trait is determined by genes within a particular population.

identical twins Twins who are genetically identical.

inspection time A measure of how long it takes an individual to perceive some simple stimulus (e.g. the longer of two lines) to a specified degree of accuracy (e.g. 90 per cent of the time).

intelligence General cognitive ability, that is, level of performance on a wide range of cognitive tasks.

neurones Nerve cells.

PET scans or Positron Emission Tomography A method of measuring which areas of the brain are most active, typically when people are solving problems.

primary mental abilities (PMAs) Thurstone's term for the factors that emerge when rather simple tests are correlated together.

reaction time A measure of how quickly a person can respond to a stimulus, e.g. pushing a button when a light comes on.

reliability A test is reliable if it has little random measurement error associated with it.

secondaries or second-order factors Factors that emerge when primary ability factors are themselves factor analysed.

unique environment Environmental influences that are not shared by any of one's brothers or sisters, e.g. friends, a relationship with a particular teacher, illness.

validity A test is valid if it measures what it claims to measure.

References

Alexander J.R.M. and Mackenzie, B.D. (1992) 'Variation of the 2-line inspection time stimulus', *Personality and Individual Differences* 13: 1201–1211.

Anderson, M. (1992) *Intelligence and Development*, Oxford: Blackwell.

Baker, L.A. and Daniels, D. (1990) 'Nonshared environmental influences and personality differences in adult twins', *Journal of Personality and Social Psychology* 58: 103–110.

Baker, L.A., Vernon, P.A. and Ho, H.-Z. (1991) 'The genetic correlation between intelligence and speed of information processing', *Behavior Genetics* 21: 351–367.

Barratt, E.S. (1995) 'History of personality and intelligence research', in D. Saklofske and M. Zeidner (eds) *International Handbook of Personality and Intelligence*, New York: Plenum.

Barrett, P.T. (1997) 'Process models in individual differences research', in C. Cooper and V. Varma (eds) *Processes in Individual Differences*, London: Routledge.

Barrett, P.T., Daum, I. and Eysenck, H.J. (1990) 'Sensory nerve conduction and intelligence: a methodological study', *Journal of Psychophysiology* 4: 1–13.

Barrett, P.T. and Eysenck, H.J. (1992) 'Brain evoked potentials and intelligence: the Hendrickson paradigm', *Intelligence* 16: 361–381.

Barrett, P.T., Eysenck, H.J. and Lucking, S. (1986) 'Reaction time and intelligence – a replicated study', *Intelligence* 10: 9–40.

Bennett, G.K. (1965) *Hand–Tool Dexterity Test*, New York: Psychological Corporation.

Bennett, G.K., Seashore, H.G. and Wesman, A.G. (1978) *Differential Aptitude Tests*, Orlando, FL: Psychological Corporation.

Bouchard, T.J.J. (1993) 'The genetic architecture of human intelligence', in P.A. Vernon (ed.) *Biological Approaches to the Study of Human Intelligence*, New York: Ablex.

Bouchard, T.J.J. (1995) 'Longitudinal studies of personality and intelligence: a behavior genetic and evolutionary psychology perspective', in D.H. Saklofske and M. Zeidner (eds) *International Handbook of Personality and Intelligence*, New York: Plenum.

Bouchard, T.J., Lykken, D.T., McGue, M., *et al.* (1990) 'Sources of human psychological differences: the Minnesota study of twins reared apart', *Science* 250: 223–228.

Bouchard, T.J.J. and McGue, M. (1981) 'Familial studies of intelligence: a review', *Science* 212: 1055–1058.

Bower, G.H. (1981) 'Mood and memory', *American Psychologist* 36: 129–148.

Brewer, N. and Smith, G.A. (1984) 'How normal and retarded individuals monitor and regulate speed and accuracy of responding in serial choice tasks', *Journal of Experimental Psychology: General* 113: 71–93.

Brody, N. (1992) *Intelligence* (2nd edn), London: Academic Press.

Brody, N. and Crowley, M.J. (1995) 'Environmental (and genetic) influences on personality and intelligence', in D.H. Saklofske and M. Zeidner (eds) *International Handbook of Personality and Intelligence*, New York: Plenum.

Carragher, T.N., Carragher, D. and Schliemann, A.D. (1985) 'Mathematics in the streets and in schools', *British Journal of Developmental Psychology* 3: 21–29.

Carroll, J.B. (1980) *Individual Difference Relations in Psychometric and Experimental Cognitive Tasks*: Report 163, Chapel Hill, NC: L.L. Thurstone Psychometric Laboratory.

Carroll, J.B. (1982) 'The measurement of intelligence', in R.J. Sternberg (ed.) *Handbook of Human Intelligence*, Cambridge: Cambridge University Press.

Carroll, J.B. (1983) 'Studying individual differences in cognitive abilities: through and beyond factor analysis', in R.F. Dillon and R.R. Schmeck (eds) *Individual Differences in Cognition vol. 1*, New York: Academic.

Carroll, J.B. (1993) *Human Cognitive Abilities: A Survey of Factor-Analytic Studies*, Cambridge: Cambridge University Press.

Carroll, J.B. (1995) 'Reflections on Stephen Jay Gould's "The Mismeasure of Man" (1981): a retrospective review', *Intelligence* 21: 121–134.

Carroll, J.B. (1997a) 'Psychometrics and public perception', *Intelligence* 24: 25–52.

Carroll, J.B. (1997b) 'Theoretical and technical issues in identifying a factor of general intelligence', in B. Devlin, S.E. Fienberg, D.P. Resnick and K. Roeder (eds) *Intelligence, Genes and Success*, New York: Springer-Verlag.

Cattell, R.B. (1971) *Abilities, their Structure Growth and Action*, New York: Houghton Mifflin.

Ceci, S. (1996) *On Intelligence*, Cambridge, MA: Harvard University Press.

Chaiken, S.R. and Young, R.K. (1993) 'Inspection time and intelligence: attempts to eliminate the apparent movements strategy', *American Journal of Psychology* 106: 191–210.

Child, D. (1990) *The Essentials of Factor Analysis*, London: Cassell.

Chipuer, H.M., Plomin, R., Pedersen, N.L., *et al.* (1993) 'Genetic influence on the family environment: the role of personality', *Developmental Psychology* 29: 110–118.

Clark, H.H. and Chase, W.G. (1972) 'On the process of comparing sentences against pictures', *Cognitive Psychology* 3: 472–517.

Cohen, J. (1988) *Statistical Power Analysis for the Social Sciences* (2nd edn), New York: Academic Press.

Comrey, A.L. and Lee, H.B. (1992) *A First Course in Factor Analysis*, Hillsdale, NJ: Lawrence Erlbaum.

Cooper, C. (1995) 'Inside the WISC-III(UK)', *Educational Psychology in Practice* 10: 215–219.

Cooper, C. (1998) *Individual Differences*, London: Arnold.

Cooper, C., Kline, P. and MacLaurin, J.L. (1986) 'Inspection time and primary abilities', *British Journal of Educational Psychology* 56: 304–308.

Crawford, J.E. and Crawford, D.M. (1956) *Small Parts Dexterity Test*, New York: Psychological Corporation.

Cronbach, L.J. (1957) 'The two disciplines of scientific psychology', *American Psychologist* 12: 671–684.

Cronbach, L.J. (1994) *Essentials of Psychological Testing*, New York: HarperCollins.

Deary, I. (1995) 'Auditory inspection time and intelligence: what is the direction of causation', *Developmental Psychology* 31: 237–250.

Deary, I.J. (1997) 'Intelligence and information processing', in H. Nyborg (ed.) *The Scientific Study of Human Nature*, Oxford: Pergamon.

Deary, I.J. and Carryl, P.G. (1993) 'Intelligence, EEG and evoked potentials', in P.A. Vernon (ed.) *Biological Approaches to the Study of Human Intelligence*, Norwood, NJ: Ablex.

Deary, I.J., Caryl, P.G., Egan, V., *et al.* (1989) 'Visual and auditory inspection time: their interrelationship and correlations with IQ in high-ability subjects', *Personality and Individual Differences* 10: 525–533.

Deary, I.J. and Stough, C. (1996) 'Intelligence and inspection time: achievements, prospects and problems', *American Psychologist* 51: 599–608.

Detterman, D.K. and Daniel, M.H. (1989) 'Correlations of mental tests with each other are highest for low IQ groups', *Intelligence* 13: 349–359.

Devlin, B., Fienberg, S.E., Resnick, D.P. and Roeder, K. (eds) (1997) *Intelligence, Genes and Success*, New York: Springer-Verlag.

DiLalla, L.F., Thompson, L.A., Plomin, R., *et al.* (1990) 'Infant predictors of pre-school and adult IQ: a study of infant twins and their parents', *Developmental Psychology* 26: 759–769.

Egan, V. (1994) 'Intelligence, inspection time and cognitive strategies', *British Journal of Psychology* 85: 305–316.

Ekstrom, R.B., French, J.W. and Harman, H.H. (1976) *Manual for the Kit of Factor-Referenced Cognitive Tests*, Princeton, NJ: Educational Testing Service.

Ertl, J.P. and Schafer, E.W.P. (1969) 'Brain response correlates of psychometric intelligence', *Nature* 223: 421–422.

Eysenck, H.J. (1953) 'The logical basis of factor analysis', *American Psychologist* 8: 105–114.

Eysenck, H.J. (1962) *Know your Own IQ*, Harmondsworth: Penguin.

Eysenck, H.J. (1967) 'Intelligence assessment: a theoretical and experimental approach', *British Journal of Educational Psychology* 37: 81–98.

Fancher, R.B. (1985) 'Spearman's computation of g: a model for Burt?', *British Journal of Psychology* 76: 341–352.

Flynn, J.R. (1987) 'Massive IQ gains in 14 nations: what IQ test really measure', *Psychological Bulletin* 101: 171–191.

Frearson, W.M., Barrett, P.T. and Eysenck, H.J. (1988) 'Intelligence, reaction time and the effects of smoking', *Personality and Individual Differences* 9: 497–517.

Frearson, W.M. and Eysenck, H.J. (1986) 'Intelligence, reaction time and a new "odd man out" paradigm', *Personality and Individual Differences* 7: 807–817.

Galton, F. (1883) *Inquiries into Human Faculty and its Development*, London: Macmillan.

Gardner, H. (1983) *Frames of Mind* (1st edn), New York: Basic Books.

Gardner, H. (1993) *Frames of Mind* (2nd edn), London: Harper-Collins.

Gasser, T., von Lucadou-Müller, I., Verleger, R. and Bächer, P. (1983) 'Correlating EEG and IQ: a new look at an old problem using computerised EEG parameters', *Electroencephalography and Clinical Neurophysiology* 55: 493–504.

Ghiselli, E.E. (1966) *The Validity of Occupational Aptitude Tests*, New York: Wiley.

Giannitrapani, D. (1969) 'EEG average frequencies and intelligence', *Electroencephalograpy and Clinical Neurophysiology* 27: 480–486.

Giannitrapani, D. (1985) *The Electrophysiology of Intellectual Functions*, Basel: S. Karger.

Gorsuch, R.L. (1983) *Factor Analysis*, Hillsdale, NJ: Lawrence Erlbaum.

Gottfredson, L.S. (1986) 'Societal consequences of the g factor in employment', *Journal of Vocational Behavior* 29: 379–410.

Gottfredson, L.S. (1997) 'Why g matters: the complexity of everyday life', *Intelligence* 24: 79–132.

Gould, S.J. (1981) *The Mismeasure of Man*, New York: Norton.

Gould, S.J. (1996) *The Mismeasure of Man: revised and expanded edition*, New York: W.W. Norton.

Guilford, J.P. (1967) *The Nature of Human Intelligence*, New York: McGraw-Hill.

Gustafsson, J.-E. (1981) 'A unifying model for the structure of intellectual abilities', *Intelligence* 8: 179–203.

Haier, R.J., Robinson, D.L., Braden, W., *et al.* (1983) 'Electrical potentials of the cerebral cortex and general intelligence', *Personality and Individual Differences* 4: 591–599.

Haier, R.J., Siegel, B., Nuechterlein, K.H., et al. (1988) 'Cortical glucose metabolic rate correlates of abstract reasoning and attention studies with positron emission tomography', *Intelligence* 12: 199–217.

Haier, R.J., Siegel, B., Tang, C., *et al.* (1992) 'Intelligence and changes in regional cerebral glucose metabolic rates following learning', *Intelligence* 12: 199–212.

Hakstian, R.N. and Cattell, R.B. (1976) *Manual for the Comprehensive Ability Battery*, Champaign, IL: Institute for Personality and Ability Testing (IPAT).

Hakstian, R.N. and Cattell, R.B. (1978) 'Higher stratum ability structure on a basis of 20 primary abilities', *Journal of Educational Psychology* 70: 657–659.

Hearnshaw, L.S. (1979) *Cyril Burt: Psychologist*, London: Hodder and Stoughton.

Heim, A.W., Watts, K.P. and Simmonds, V. (1970) *AH4, AH5 and AH6 Tests*, Windsor: NFER.

Hendrickson, A.E. (1982a) 'The biological basis of intelligence. Part 1: theory', in H.J. Eysenck (ed.) *A Model for Intelligence*, Berlin: Springer-Verlag.

Hendrickson, D.E. (1982b) 'The biological basis of intelligence. Part II: measurement', in H.J. Eysenck (ed.) *A Model for Intelligence*, Berlin: Springer-Verlag.

Herrnstein, R.J. and Murray, C. (1994) *The Bell Curve: Intelligence and Class Structure in American Life*, New York: The Free Press.

Horn, J.L. and Cattell, R.B. (1966) 'Refinement and test of the theory of fluid and crystallised intelligence', *Journal of Educational Psychology* 57: 253–270.

Howe, M.J.A. (1988a) 'The hazard of using correlational evidence as a means of identifying the causes of individual ability differences: a rejoinder to Sternberg and a reply to Miles', *British Journal of Psychology* 79: 539–545.

Howe, M.J.A. (1988b) 'Intelligence as explanation', *British Journal of Psychology* 79: 349–360.

Howe, M.J.A. (1989) *Fragments of Genius*, London: Routledge.

Howe, M.J.A. (1997) *IQ in Question: The Truth About Intelligence*, London: Sage.

Howe, M.J.A. (1998) 'Can IQ change?', *The Psychologist* 11: 69–72.

Hunt, E. (1995a) 'The role of intelligence in modern society', *American Scientist*: via Internet.

Hunt, E. (1995b) *Will We be Smart Enough? A Cognitive Analysis of the Coming Workforce*, New York: Russell Sage Foundation.

Hunt, E.B. (1978) 'The mechanics of verbal ability', *Psychological Review* 85: 109–130.

Hunter, J.E. (1986) 'Cognitive ability, cognitive attitudes, job knowledge and job performance', *Journal of Vocational Behavior* 29: 340–362.

Hunter, J.E. and Hunter, R.F. (1984) 'Validity and utility of alternative predictors of job performance', *Psychological Bulletin* 96: 72–98.

Jacoby, R. and Glauberman, N. (eds) (1995) *The Bell Curve Debate: History, Documents, Opinions*, New York: Times Books.

Jensen, A.R. (1977) 'Genetic and behavioral effects of non-random mating', in C.E. Noble, R.T. Osborne and N. Weyl (eds) *Human Variation: Biogenetics of Age, Race and Sex*, New York: Academic Press.

Jensen, A.R. (1987) 'Individual differences in the Hick paradigm', in P.A. Vernon (ed.) *Speed of Information-Processing and Intelligence*, Norwood, NJ: Ablex.

Jensen, A.R. (1993) 'Spearman's g: links between psychometrics and biology', *Annals of the New York Academy of Sciences* 702: 103–129.

Jensen, A.R. (1997) 'The psychophysiology of g', in C. Cooper and V. Varma (eds) *Process Models of Individual Differences*, London: Routledge.

Jensen, A.R. (1998) *The g Factor*, New York: Praeger.

Jensen, A.R. and Munroe, E. (1974) 'Reaction time, movement time and intelligence', *Intelligence* 3: 121–126.

Jensen, A.R. and Sinha, S.N. (1993) 'Physical correlates of human intelligence', in P.A. Vernon (ed.) *Biological Approaches to the Study of Human Intelligence*, Norwood, NJ: Ablex.

Jinks, J.L. and Fulker, D.W. (1970) 'Comparison of the biometrical genetical, MAVA and classsical approaches to the analysis of human behavior', *Psychological Bulletin* 73: 311–349.

Kamin, L.J. (1974) *The Science and Politics of IQ*, Harmondsworth: Penguin.

Kamin, L.J. (1995) 'Lies, damned lies and statistics', in R. Jacoby and N. Glauberman (eds) *The Bell Curve Debate: History, Documents, Opinions*, New York: Times Books.

Kanfer, P.L., Ackerman, Y.M. and Goff, M. (1995) 'Personality and intelligence in industrial and organizational psychology', in D.H. Saklofske and M. Zeidner (eds) *International Handbook of Personality and Intelligence*, New York: Plenum.

Katsanis, J., Iacono, W.G., McGue, M.K., *et al.* (1997) 'P300 event-related potential heritability in monozygotic and dizygotic twins', *Psychophysiology* 34: 47–58.

Kline, P. (1986) *A handbook of Test Construction*, London: Methuen.

Kline, P. (1991) *Intelligence: The Psychometric View*, London: Routledge.

Kline, P. (1993) The Handbook of Psychological Testing, London: Routledge.

Kline, P. (1994) *An Easy Guide to Factor Analysis*, London: Routledge.

Kranzler, J.H. and Jensen, A.R. (1989) 'Inspection time and intelligence: a meta-analysis', *Intelligence* 13: 329–347.

Larson, G.E. and Alderton, D.L. (1990) 'Reaction-time variability and intelligence: "worst performance" analysis of individual differences', *Intelligence* 14: 309–325.

Larson, G.E., Haier, R.J., LaCasse, L., *et al.* (1995) 'Evaluation of a 'mental effort' hypothesis for correlations between cortical metabolism and intelligence', *Intelligence* 21: 267–278.

Levy, P. (1992) 'Inspection time and its relation to intelligence: issues of measurement and meaning', *Personality and Individual Differences* 13: 987–1002.

Loehlin, J.C., Horn, J.M. and Willerman, L. (1989) 'Modeling IQ change: evidence from the Texas Adoption Project', *Child Development* 60: 993–1004.

Longstreth, L.E. (1984) 'Jensen's reaction time investigations: a critique', *Intelligence* 8: 139–160.

Longstreth, L.E. (1986) 'The real and the unreal: a reply to Jensen and Vernon', *Intelligence* 10: 181–191.

Mackintosh, N.J. (1995) 'Insight into intelligence', *Nature* 377: 581–582.

Matthews, G. and Dorn, L. (1995) 'Cognitive and attentional processes in personality and intelligence', in D.H. Saklofske and M. Zeidner (eds) *International Handbook of Personality and Intelligence*, New York: Plenum.

May, J., Kline, P. and Cooper, C. (1987) 'A brief computerized form of a schematic analogy task', *British Journal of Psychology* 78: 29–36.

Moos, R.H. and Moos, B.S. (1981) *Family Environment Scale Manual*, Palo Alto, CA: Consulting Psychologists Press.

Mulhern, G.A. (1997) 'Intelligence and cognitive processing', in C. Cooper and V. Varma (eds) *Processes in Individual Differences*, London: Routledge.

Mundy-Castle, A.C. (1958) 'Electrophysiological correlates of intelligence', *Journal of Personality* 26: 184–199.

Neisser, U. (1983) 'Components of intelligence or steps in routine procedures?', *Cognition* 15: 189–197.

Neisser, U., Boodoo, G., Bouchard, T., *et al.* (1996) 'Intelligence: knowns and unknowns', *American Psychologist* 51: 77–101.

Nettelbeck, T. (1982) 'Inspection time: an index for intelligence', *Quarterly Journal of Experimental Psychology* 34: 299–312.

Nettelbeck, T. (1987) 'Inspection time and intelligence', in P.A. Vernon (ed.) *Speed of Information Processing and Intelligence*, Norwood, NJ: Ablex.

Nettelbeck, T. and Kirby, N.H. (1983) 'Measures of timed performance and intelligence', *Intelligence* 7: 39–52.

Nettelbeck, T. and Lally, M. (1976) 'Inspection time and measured intelligence', *British Journal of Psychology* 67: 17–22.

Nunnally, J.C. (1978) *Psychometric Theory*, New York: McGraw-Hill.

O'Gorman, J.G. and Lloyd, J.E.M. (1985) 'Is EEG a consistent measure of individual differences?', *Personality and Individual Differences* 6: 273–275.

Palermo, J.B. (1964) *The Computer Programmer Aptitude Battery* (CPAB), Chicago, IL: Science Research Associates.

Parks, R.W., Loewenstein, D.A., Dodrill, K.L., *et al.* (1988) 'Cerebral metabolic effects of a verbal fluency test: a PET scan study', *Journal of Clinical and Experimental Neuropsychology* 10: 565–575.

Pedersen, N. and Lichtenstein, P. (1997) 'Biometric analyses of human abilities', in C. Cooper and V. Varma (eds) *Processes in Individual Differences*, London: Routledge.

Petrill, S.A., Luo, D., Thompson, L.A., *et al.* (1996) 'The independent prediction of general intelligence by elementary cognitive tasks: genetic influences', *Behavior Genetics* 26: 135–147.

Plomin, R., Campos, J., Corley, R., *et al.* (1990) 'Individual differences within the second year of life: the MacArthur Longitudinal Twin Study', in J. Columbo and J. Fagan (eds) *Individual Differences in Infancy: Reliability, Stability and Predictability*, Hillsdale, NJ: Lawrence Erlbaum.

Plomin, R. and Daniels, D. (1987) 'Why are children in the same family so different from one another?', *Behavioral and Brain Science* 10: 1–16.

Plomin, R., Loehlin, J.C. and DeFries, J.C. (1985) 'Genetic and environmental components of "environmental" influences', *Developmental Psychology* 21: 391–402.

Plomin, R. and McClearn, G.E. (eds) (1993) *Nature, Nurture and Psychology*, Washington, DC: American Psychological Association.

Plomin, R. and McClearn, G.E. (1990) 'Human behavioral genetics of aging', in J.E. Birren and K.W. Schaie (eds) *Handbook of the Psychology of Aging*, (3rd edn), San Diego, CA: Academic Press.

Plomin, R., McClearn, G.E., Skuder, P., et al. (1995) 'Allelic associations between 100 DNA markers and high versus low IQ', *Intelligence* 21: 31–48.

Plomin, R. and Petrill, S.A. (1997) 'Genetics and intelligence: what's new?', *Intelligence* 24: 53–77.

Posner, M.I. (1980) 'Ordering of attention', *Quarterly Journal of Experimental Psychology* 32: 3–25.

Posner, M.I. and Mitchell, R. (1967) 'Chronometric analysis of classification', *Psychological Review* 74: 392–409.

Posner, M.I., Petersen, S.E., Fox, P.T., *et al.* (1988) 'Localization of cognitive operations in the human brain', *Science* 240: 1627–1631.

Rabbitt, P.M.A. (1985) 'Oh g Dr Jensen! Or, g-ing up cognitive psychology', *Behavioral and Brain Sciences* 8: 238–239.

Raven, J.C. (1965) *Advanced Progressive Matrices*, London: H.K. Lewis.

Reed, T.E. and Jensen, A.R. (1991) 'Arm nerve conduction velocity (NCV), brain NCV, reaction time and intelligence', *Intelligence* 15: 33–47.

Richardson, K. (1991) *Understanding Intelligence*, Milton Keynes: Open University Press.

Rijsdijk, F.V., Boonsma, F.V. and Vernon, P.A. (1995) 'Genetic analysis of peripheral nerve conduction velocity in twins', *Behavior Genetics* 25: 341–348.

Robinson, D.L. (1996) *Brain, Mind, and Behavior: A New Perspective on Human Nature*, Westport, CT: Praeger.

Rogers, C.R. (1959) 'A theory of therapy, personality and interpersonal relationships, as developed in the client-centered framework', in S. Koch (ed.) *Psychology: A Study of a Science*, New York: McGraw-Hill.

Rose, S., Lewontin, R.C. and Kamin, L.J. (1984) *Not in our Genes*, Harmondsworth: Penguin.

Rowe, D.C. (1997) 'A place at the policy table?', *Intelligence* 24: 133–158.

Rust, J. (1975) 'Cortical evoked potential, personality and intelligence', *Journal of Comparative and Physiological Psychology* 89: 1220–1226.

Scarr, S. and Carter-Saltzman, L. (1982) 'Genetics and intelligence', in R.J. Sternberg (ed.) *Handbook of Human Intelligence*, Cambridge: Cambridge University Press.

Segal, N. (1997) 'Same-age unrelated siblings: a unique test of within-family environmental influences on IQ similarity', *Journal of Educational Psychology* 89: 381–390.

Skodak, M. and Skeels, H.M. (1949) 'A final follow-up study of one hundred adopted children', *Journal of Genetic Psychology* 75: 85–125.

Snyderman, M. and Rothman, S. (1987) 'Survey of expert opinion on intelligence and aptitude testing', *American Psychologist* 42: 137–144.

Sokal, R.R. and Sneath, P.H. (1963) *Principles of Numeric Taxonomy*, London: W.H. Freeman.

Spearman, C. (1904) 'General intelligence objectively determined and measured', *American Journal of Psychology* 15: 201–293.

Stelmack, R.M. and Houlihan, M. (1995) 'Event-related potentials, personality and intelligence: concepts, issues and evidence', in D.H. Saklofske and M. Zeidner (eds) *International Handbook of Personality and Intelligence*, New York: Plenum.

Sternberg, R.J. (1977) *Intelligence, Information Processing and Analogical Reasoning: the Componential Analysis of Human Abilities*, Hillsdale, NJ: Erlbaum.

Sternberg, R.J. (1985) *Beyond IQ*, Cambridge: Cambridge University Press.

Sternberg, R.J. (1988) 'Explaining away intelligence: a reply to Howe', *British Journal of Psychology* 79: 527–534.

Sternberg, R.J. and Gardner, M.K. (1983) 'Unities in inductive reasoning', *Journal of Experimental Psychology*: General 112: 80–116.

Sternberg, R.J. and Salter, W. (1982) 'Conceptions of intelligence', in R.J. Sternberg (ed.) *Handbook of Human Intelligence*, Cambridge: Cambridge University Press.

Sternberg, R.J. and Wagner, R.K. (1986) *Practical Intelligence: the Nature and Origins of Competence in the Everyday World*, Cambridge: Cambridge University Press.

Sternberg, S. (1969) 'High-speed scanning in human memory', *Science* 153: 652–654.

REFERENCES

Stevenson, J. (1997) 'The genetic basis of personality', in C. Cooper and V. Varma (eds) *Processes in Individual Differences*, London: Routledge.

Stroop, J.R. (1935) 'Studies of interference in serial verbal reactions', *Journal of Experimental Psychology* 18: 643–662.

Sundet, J.M., Tambs, K., Magnus, P. and Berg, K. (1988) 'On the question of secular trends in the heritability of intelligence test scores: a study of Norwegian twins', *Intelligence* 12: 47–59.

Thompson, L.A. (1993) 'Genetic contributions to intellectual development in infancy and childhood', in P.A. Vernon (ed.) *Biological Approaches to the Study of Human Intelligence*, Norwood, NJ: Ablex.

Thorndike, E.L. (1921) 'Intelligence and its measurement: a symposium', *Journal of Educational Psychology* 12: 123–147, 195–216, 271–275.

Thorndike, R.L. (1985) 'The central role of general ability in prediction', *Multivariate Behavioral Research* 20: 241–254.

Thurstone, L.L. (1938) *Primary Mental Abilities*, Chicago: University of Chicago Press.

Thurstone, L.L. (1947) *Multiple Factor Analysis: A Development and Expansion of the Vectors of Mind*, Chicago: University of Chicago Press.

Tryon, R.C. (1940) 'Genetic differences in maze-learning ability in rats', *Yearbook of the National Society of Student Education* 39: 111–119.

Undheim, J.O. (1981) 'On intelligence I: broad ability factors in 15 year old children and Cattell's theory of fluid and crystallised intelligence', *Scandinavian Journal of Psychology* 22: 171–179.

United States Employment Service (USES) (1979) *Manual for the USES General Aptitude Test Battery*, Washington, DC: US Government Printing Office.

Vernon, P.A. (1990) 'An overview of chronometric measures of intelligence', *School Psychology Review* 19: 499–410.

Vernon, P.A. and Mori, M. (1992) 'Intelligence, reaction times and peripheral nerve conduction velocity', *Intelligence* 16: 273–288.

Vernon, P.E. (1950) *Structure of Human Abilities*, London: Methuen.

Vernon, P.E. (1961) *The Measurement of Abilities*, London: University of London Press.

Vernon, P.E. (1979) *Intelligence, Heredity and Environment*, San Francisco CA: W.J. Freeman.

172

Vickers, D., Nettelbeck, T. and Willson, R.J. (1972) 'Perceptual indices of performance: the measurement of "inspection time" and "noise" in the visual system', *Perception* 1: 264–295.

Weiss, V. (1986) 'From memory span and mental speed towards the quantum mechanics of intelligence', *Personality and Individual Differences* 7: 737–749.

Weiss, V. (1989) 'From short-term memory capacity toward the EEG resonance code', *Personality and Individual Differences* 10: 501–508

Weschler, D. (1974) *WAIS-R Manual*, New York: Psychological Corporation.

White, K.R. (1982) 'The relationship between socioeconomic status and academic achievement', *Psychological Bulletin* 81: 461–481.

White, M. (1996) 'Interpreting inspection time as a measure of the speed of sensory processing', *Personality and Individual Differences* 20: 351–363.

Wickett, J.C. and Vernon, P.A. (1994) 'Peripheral nerve conduction velocity, reaction time, and intelligence: an attempt to replicate Vernon and Mori (1992)', *Intelligence* 18: 127–131.

Widaman, K.F. and Carlson, J.S. (1989) 'Procedural effects on performance in the Hick paradigm: bias in reaction time and movement parameters', *Intelligence* 13: 63–85.

Willis, W.G. and Aspel, A.D. (1994) 'Neuropsychological models of information processing: a framework for evaluation', in P.A. Vernon (ed.) *The Neuropsychology of Individual Differences*, London: Academic Press.

Wilson, R.C. (1983) 'The Louisville Twin Study: developmental synchronies in behavior', *Child Development* 54: 298–316.

Index